Test Yourself

Physics I

M. Azad Islam, Ph.D.
Department of Physics
State University of New York, Potsdam
Potsdam, NY

Contributing Editors

Christopher J. Cramer, Ph.D.
Department of Chemistry
University of Minnesota
Minneapolis, MN

Kelly B. Knowlton, Ph.D.
Department of Chemistry, Physics, and Geology
Northwestern State University of Louisiana
Natchitoches, LA

Frederick C. Thatcher, Ph.D.
Department of Physics
Indiana University–Purdue University at Indianapolis
Indianapolis, IN

NTC LearningWorks
NTC/Contemporary Publishing Group

Library of Congress Cataloging-in-Publication Data

Islam, M. Azad.
    Physics I / M. Azad Islam ; contributing editors, Christopher J.
Cramer, Kelly B. Knowlton, Frederick C. Thatcher.
      p. cm. — (Test yourself)
    ISBN 0-8442-2377-8
    1. Physics—Problems, exercises, etc. 2. Physics—Ability
testing.   I. Cramer, Christopher J., 1961– .   II. Knowlton, Kelly B.
III. Thatcher, Frederick C.   IV. Title.   V. Series: Test
yourself (Lincolnwood, Ill.)
QC20.82.I85   1997
531'.076—dc21   97-25168
                                                                                   CIP

This book is dedicated to my parents, Haji Mohsin Ali and Amena Khatun,
who made education their first choice for opportunity and progress of their eight children.

A *Test Yourself Books, Inc.* **Project**

Published by NTC LearningWorks
A division of NTC/Contemporary Publishing Group, Inc.
4255 West Touhy Avenue, Lincolnwood (Chicago), Illinois 60646-1975 U.S.A.
Copyright © 1999 by NTC/Contemporary Publishing Group, Inc.
All rights reserved. No part of this book may be reproduced, stored
in a retrieval system, or transmitted in any form or by any means,
electronic, mechanical, photocopying, recording, or otherwise, without
the prior permission of NTC/Contemporary Publishing Group, Inc.
Printed in the United States of America
International Standard Book Number: 0-8442-2377-8
18 17 16 15 14 13 12 11 10 9 8 7 6 5 4 3 2 1

Contents

Preface v

How to Use This Book... vii

1. Measurement and Analysis 1
2. Motion in One Dimension 13
3. Vectors 27
4. Motion in Two Dimensions 38
5. Force and Motion 58
6. Work and Energy 78
7. Momentum and Impulse 92
8. Rotational Motion 109
9. Objects in Equilibrium 122
10. Fluid Mechanics 139
11. Temperature, Heat, and Thermodynamics 159
12. Vibrations and Wave Motion 174

Preface

Present day introductory physics textbooks are usually voluminous and students have a hard time mastering all the material for closed-book tests. The need to become familiar with only a handful of formulas and equations to tackle all the problems in a chapter should be very attractive to all students. Most physicists train themselves with a set of basic principles and laws of nature that they apply to solve a variety of real-world problems. This book provides a bare-bones structure to engage students in solving all of the problems in their texts. This book has been written with students in mind—students who have studied the textbook and are ready to try their skills at scoring high on quizzes and exams.

This book covers all the principal topics taught in an introductory physics course, from mechanics to thermodynamics. There are four parts in each chapter of this book. The first part, Brief Yourself, is a brief discussion of the principles and formulas in a chapter. The second part, Test Yourself, consists of typical problems that students will encounter in a test situation. A student should try to solve all of the problems with only the formulas in the chapter in mind. Occasionally, one or more formulas from the previous chapters may be necessary to solve a problem completely. After completion of the practice test, each student must carefully check his or her answers and the solutions provided in the third part, Check Yourself. In the fourth part, Grade Yourself, students circle the incorrect answers to help identify their strengths and weaknesses.

I would like to thank Fred Grayson for recognizing the students' predicament in a test situation and for providing me the opportunity to write a book to help students improve their performance on all their tests.

M. Azad Islam, Ph.D.

How to Use This Book

This "Test Yourself" book is part of a unique series designed to help you improve your test scores on almost any type of examination you will face. Too often, you will study for a test—quiz, midterm, or final—and come away with a score that is lower than anticipated. Why? Because there is no way for you to really know how much you understand a topic until you've taken a test. The *purpose* of the test, after all, is to test your complete understanding of the material.

The "Test Yourself" series offers you a way to improve your scores and to actually test your knowledge at the time you use this book. Consider each chapter a diagnostic pretest in a specific topic. Answer the questions, check your answers, and then give yourself a grade. Then, and only then, will you know where your strengths and, more important, weaknesses are. Once these areas are identified, you can strategically focus your study on those topics that need additional work.

Each book in this series presents a specific subject in an organized manner, and although each "Test Yourself" chapter may not correspond to exactly the same chapter in your textbook, you should have little difficulty in locating the specific topic you are studying. Written by educators in the field, each book is designed to correspond, as much as possible, to the leading textbooks. This means that you can feel confident in using this book, and that regardless of your textbook, professor, or school, you will be much better prepared for anything you will encounter on your test.

Each chapter has four parts:

Brief Yourself. All chapters contain a brief overview of the topic that is intended to give you a more thorough understanding of the material with which you need to be familiar. Sometimes this information is presented at the beginning of the chapter, and sometimes it flows throughout the chapter, to review your understanding of various *units* within the chapter.

Test Yourself. Each chapter covers a specific topic corresponding to one that you will find in your textbook. Answer the questions, either on a separate page or directly in the book, if there is room.

Check Yourself. Check your answers. Every question is fully answered and explained. These answers will be the key to your increased understanding. If you answered the question incorrectly, read the explanations to *learn* and *understand* the material. You will note that at the end of every answer you will be referred to a specific subtopic within that chapter, so you can focus your studying and prepare more efficiently.

Grade Yourself. At the end of each chapter is a self-diagnostic key. By indicating on this form the numbers of those questions you answered incorrectly, you will have a clear picture of your weak areas.

There are no secrets to test success. Only good preparation can guarantee higher grades. By utilizing this "Test Yourself" book, you will have a better chance of improving your scores and understanding the subject more fully.

Measurement and Analysis

 Brief Yourself

Physics, a Greek word meaning knowledge of the natural world, has a well-organized formalism. Learning physics is much like learning about a new culture. In physics, scientific notations are widely used. A number such as 0.0235 is likely to be written in powers of 10. You need to learn the symbols and notations. Simple models are constructed to explain the complex behavior of physical systems. Physicists try to explain the models in mathematical terms. Such models backed by mathematical expressions, however, must contain measurable physical quantities.

Physics is an experimental science in which quantities are measured and analyzed. This entails some basic knowledge of mathematics. Learning basic physics invariably means learning to manipulate algebraic expressions in simple steps and analyzing the given conditions and/or data of a stated problem. For introductory physics, this requires becoming familiar with some of the fundamental rules of mathematics. For example, while solving a problem you may have to use the theorem of Pythagoras ($a^2 + b^2 = c^2$) or use trigonometry (such as $\tan\theta = y/x$). Many times, angles are measured in radians ($\theta = s/r$), where $180° = \pi$ radians. Knowledge of the expressions for circumference ($2\pi r$), area of a circle (πr^2) and volume of a cylinder ($\pi r^2 L$), to name a few, will be quite useful in solving problems.

All physical quantities can be expressed in terms of three fundamental quantities: length, mass, and time. These are expressed in terms of meter (m), kilogram (kg) and second (s) in the International System (SI) of units. Another system of units is called the cgs or Gaussian system. In the cgs system of units, length, mass, and time are expressed in terms of centimeter (cm), gram (g), and second (s). In the British engineering system, length, mass, and time are expressed in terms of foot, slug, and second, respectively.

Sometimes it is necessary to convert SI units into other units or vice versa (for example, converting foot and slug into meter and kilogram). The physical quantities that are measured and expressed come in a variety of units. Except for the three fundamental units mentioned above, the rest are called derived units (e.g., newton, the unit of force).

Frequently, approximate values of many physical quantities are of greater interest than finding the exact answer, which may involve cumbersome calculations. Whenever an approximate or order of magnitude calculation is made, the results are generally reliable within a factor of 10. A quantity that increases its value by three orders of magnitude is increased 1,000 times.

Dimensional analysis is a powerful tool for verifying the validity of formulas and expressions. Dimension means the physical nature of a quantity. Dimensional analysis treats all dimensions as algebraic quantities. The individual units of a formula are often analyzed to check the correctness of an equation. Quantities can be added or subtracted only if their dimensions are the same. Whenever individual dimensions are analyzed in a mathematical expression, dimensions of each side of the equation must be the same. Each of the terms appearing in the equation must also have the same unit.

When using many quantities in a calculation, the quantity with the least significant digits will determine the significant figures of the final result. When multiplying or dividing two or more quantities, the number of significant figures in the final answer will be the same as the quantity with the least number of significant digits used in the calculation.

Test Yourself

1. Write down the following quantities in scientific notations.

    (a) 321.8
    (b) 0.00304
    (c) 60108
    (d) 50003

2. Express the following quantities in simple numbers without the exponent.

    (a) 53.73×10^{-4}
    (b) $1/(4.05 \times 10^{-3})$
    (c) $1/63 \times 10^{-2}$
    (d) 0.023×10^{6}

3. You run 40 meters north and then turn right and run 30 meters east. Finally, you return to your initial position in a straight line. What is the straight line distance you traveled last?

4. The volume of a cube is 1×10^{-6} m³. What is the length of the side?

5. The result of the following calculation

    $[(3.61 \times 10^{5})/(8.347 \times 10^{-2})] \times 4.6 \times 10^{-7}$ is:

    (a) 1.98×10^{-13}
    (b) 1.984×10^{14}
    (c) 1.984×10^{2}
    (d) 1.984

6. Find the results of the following calculations.

    (a) $(C \times 10^{n}) \times (D \times 10^{m})$
    (b) $(A \times 10^{a})/(B \times 10^{b})$
    (c) $[(C^{n}) \times (D^{m})]^{s}$

7. In a total solar eclipse, the moon's shadow just overlaps the sun. The distance from the Earth to the sun is 1.5×10^{11} m and the distance from the Earth to the moon is 3.8×10^{8} m. Estimate the relative diameter of the sun and the moon.

8. Through how many radians does the Earth turn on its own axis in one year?

9. While trying to draw a perfect circle of radius 2.5 cm, Mary drew three quarters of a circle in one try.

    (a) Through how many radians has she drawn?
    (b) What is the perimeter of this unfinished circle?

10. An imperfect wall clock loses 1.5 seconds every day. How slow will it be in two years?

11. How many cubic centimeters are there in one cubic foot?

12. A U.S. student traveling in India finds the cost of a radio to be 800 rupees in Indian currency. Find

the cost of the radio in U.S. dollars if the rate of conversion that day is 28 rupees for $1.

13. The speed of light is 186,000 miles per second. Find the speed in:

    (a) miles per hour
    (b) meters per second.

14. A car is running at 60 miles per hour. Convert the speed to meters per second.

15. Federal law allows cars to run at 65 miles per hour on the freeways. How much is the increase in kilometers per hour over the old speed limit of 55 miles per hour?

16. An Egyptian pyramid contains approximately 2 million stone blocks. The weight of each block is about 2.5 metric tons. Find the weight of the pyramids in pounds.

17. Gasoline sells at $1.35 per gallon in the United States. What is the price per liter?

    1 gallon = 3.7853 liters

18. An acre is equal to 43,560 ft². How many square meters will fit in a plot of land one acre in area?

19. How far will laser light go in one nanosecond? Speed of light is 3×10^8 m/s in a vacuum.

20. A water tank contains 100 cu. ft. of water. What is the volume in cubic meters?

21. Use proper prefixes to name the following:

    (a) 5×10^{-3} m
    (b) 4×10^{-6} s
    (c) 2×10^3 g
    (d) 8×10^{-9} m

22. Density is stated in kg/m³. Use dimensional analysis to verify the unit of volume of a cylindrical solid object.

23. Distance "x" traveled by a car is $x = at^2$, where t stands for time. What is the unit of acceleration "a"?

24. Speed "u" and acceleration "a" are stated in m/s and m/s², respectively. Use the following equation to find the unit of the distance "x."

$u^2 = u_0^2 + 2ax$ (u_0 is the initial speed)

25. The constant π is approximately equal to 3.141593. What is the value in four significant figures?

    (a) 3.1416
    (b) 3.142
    (c) 3.14
    (d) 3.143

26. The number 0.04614 has the following number of significant figures.

    (a) 4
    (b) 5
    (c) 6
    (d) 3

27. A surveyor measures a rectangular plot of land and finds the length to be 41.22 m and the width to be 25.49 m. Calculate the area in the most significant figures.

28. Calculate the volume of a rectangular block of wood in the most significant figures if its length is 105 cm, width 26.8 cm, and height 2.6 cm.

29. Bangladesh, one of the most densely populated nations in the world, has a population of 119 million people in 55,000 square miles. What is the density of population (in the most significant figures) in that country?

30. The thickness of the page of a textbook is 5×10^{-3} cm. If the textbook is 3.4 cm high, find the number of pages in the textbook in the most significant figures.

31. Find the volume in the most significant figures of a rectangular parallelepiped whose dimensions are $5.2 \times 3.925 \times 2.25$ m³.

32. The speed of light is known to be 2.997924×10^8 m/s. Write this speed in three and four significant figures.

33. A solid piece of metal has a mass of 55 g and a volume of 2.85 cc. Calculate the density of this metal in the most significant figures in SI units.

34. A cake in the shape of a rectangular parallelepiped measures 12 in × 18 in × 3 in. Find the volume in most significant figures in SI units.

35. A painter is painting the 4 walls of a room 10.0 ft. high and 15.0 ft. along each side. Calculate the total area (including the ceiling), in most significant figures in sq. meters, he has to paint. (Ignore the area of doors and windows)

36. How many heartbeats will a person undergo in a lifetime of 75 years? Average heart rate is 70 pulses/min.

37. Calculate the approximate volume of a Coke can with a diameter of 6 cm and a length of 12 cm.

38. The order of magnitude of the thickness of a dime is:

    (a) 10^{-6} m
    (b) 10^{-3} m
    (c) 10^{-2} m
    (d) 10^{-4} m

39. The number of minutes in one year for order of magnitude calculation is:

    (a) 10^3 min
    (b) 10^8 min
    (c) 10^5 min
    (d) 10^4 min

40. Estimate the amount of toothpaste used and its cost in the United States per year. (Mass of a tube of toothpaste = 170 g, cost = $1.50, number of households in the United States = 60 million, and each household uses two tubes per month.)

41. Estimate the amount of motor oil used and its cost in the United States per year. There are 120 million cars in the United States, the mass of a can of motor oil is 450 g, each can costs $1.20, and each car runs 12,000 miles per year. Assume each car has an oil change every 3,000 miles, using 5 cans of motor oil per oil change.

Check Yourself

1. (a) 3.218×10^2

   (b) 3.04×10^{-3}

   (c) 6.0108×10^4

   (d) 5.0003×10^4 **(Measurement)**

2. (a) 0.005373

   (b) 246.9

   (c) 0.000159

   (d) 23000   **(Measurement)**

3. Using the theorem of Pythagoras,

   $x^2 = 40^2 + 30^2 = 1{,}600 + 900 = 2{,}500$

   $x = 50$ m   **(Measurement)**

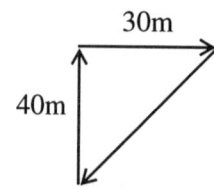

4. Volume of a cube, $V = x^3$

   $x = (V)^{1/3} = (1 \times 10^{-6} \text{ m}^3)^{1/3}$

$$x = (1\times10^{-6})^{1/3} \, (m^3)^{1/3}$$

$$x = \left(1\times10^{-\frac{6\times1}{3}}\right)\left(m^{3\times\frac{1}{3}}\right)$$

$$x = (1\times10^{-2}) \, m^1$$

$x = 1\times10^{-2}$ m = 1 cm, is the length of a side. **(Measurement)**

5. $\left(\dfrac{3.61\times10^5}{8.347\times10^{-2}}\right) \times (4.6\times10^{-7})$

   $= \dfrac{3.61\times10^7}{8.347} \times 4.6\times10^{-7}$

   $= \dfrac{3.61 \times 4.6 \times 10^0}{8.347}$

   $= \dfrac{3.61 \times 4.6}{8.347}$

   $= 1.984$ **(Measurement)**

6. (a) $C \times D \times 10^{m+n}$

   (b) $(A/B) \times 10^{a-b}$

   (c) $(C^{n\times s})(D^{m\times s})$ **(Measurement)**

7.

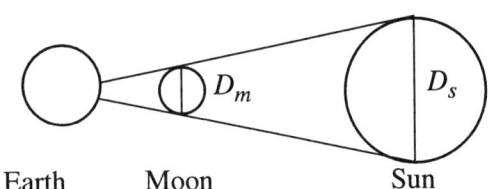

Earth   Moon   Sun

Using the law of equivalent triangles:

$\dfrac{D_s}{D_m} = \dfrac{1.5\times10^{11}}{3.8\times10^8} = 3.95\times10^2 = 395$ **(Measurement)**

8. Each day, one turn = 2π radians

   365 turns in one year.

   Each year = $2\pi \times 365 = 730\,\pi$ radians   **(Measurement)**

9.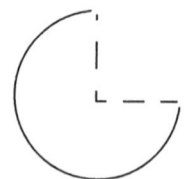

(a) Full circle = 2π radians

$\frac{3}{4}$ circle = $2\pi \times \frac{3}{4}$ = 1.5π radians

(b) Circumference of a circle = $2\pi r$

Perimeter of $\frac{3}{4}$ circle = $2\pi r \times \frac{3}{4}$ = $1.5\pi r$

$= 1.5 \times \pi \times 2.5$
$= 11.8$ cm

(Measurement)

10. Each day, 1.5s

Each year, $1.5 \times 365 = 547.5$ s

Two years $= 547.5 \times 2 = 1.095 \times 10^3$ s

$= 18.2$ minutes   **(Measurement)**

11. 1 cu. ft. = 1 ft × 1 ft × 1 ft

$= (12 \text{ in}) \times (12 \text{ in}) \times (12 \text{ in})$

$= (12 \times 2.54 \text{ cm}) \times (12 \times 2.54 \text{ cm}) \times (12 \times 2.54 \text{ cm})$

$= 2.83 \times 10^4$ cm^3 **(Units and standards)**

12. $1 = 28 rupees

1 rupee = $\frac{1}{28}$ dollars

800 rupees = $\frac{1}{28} \times 800 = \$28.57$ **(Units and standards)**

13. (a) $186,000 \frac{\text{mi}}{\text{s}} = 186,000 \frac{\text{mi}}{\text{s}} \left(\frac{60 \text{s}}{1 \text{ min}}\right)$

$= \frac{186,000 \times 60 \text{ mi}}{\text{min}}$

$= \frac{186,000 \times 60 \text{ (mi)}}{\text{min}} \left(\frac{60 \text{ min}}{1 \text{ hr}}\right)$

$$= \frac{186,000 \times 60 \times 60 \text{ (mi)}}{\text{hr}}$$

$$= 6.696 \times 10^8 \text{ mi/hr}$$

(b) $186,000 \frac{\text{mi}}{\text{s}} = 186,000 \times \left(\frac{1760 \text{ yds}}{1 \text{ mi}}\right)\frac{\text{mi}}{\text{s}}$

$$= 186,000 \times 1760 \left(\frac{\text{yds}}{\text{s}}\right) \times \left(\frac{3 \text{ ft}}{1 \text{ yd}}\right)$$

$$= 186,000 \times 1760 \times 3 \times \left(\frac{12 \text{ in}}{1 \text{ ft}}\right)\frac{\text{ft}}{\text{s}} \times \left(\frac{2.54 \times 10^{-2} \text{ m}}{1 \text{ in}}\right)$$

$$= 186,000 \times 1760 \times 3 \times 12 \times 2.54 \times 10^{-2} \text{ m/s}$$

$$= 2.993 \times 10^8 \text{ m/s} \quad \textbf{(Units and standards)}$$

14. $60 \frac{\text{mi}}{\text{hr}} = 60\left(\frac{\text{mi}}{\text{hr}}\right)\frac{1760 \text{ yd}}{1 \text{ mi}} \times \frac{3 \text{ ft}}{1 \text{ yd}} \times \frac{12 \text{ in}}{1 \text{ ft}} \times \frac{2.54 \times 10^{-2} \text{ m}}{1 \text{ in}}$

$$= 60 \times 1760 \times 3 \times 12 \times 2.54 \times 10^{-2} \text{ m/hr}$$

$$= 9.656 \times 10^4 \left(\frac{\text{m}}{\text{hr}}\right)\frac{1 \text{ hr}}{60 \text{ min}} \times \left(\frac{1 \text{ min}}{60 \text{ s}}\right)$$

$$= \frac{9.656 \times 10^4}{60 \times 60} \frac{\text{m}}{\text{s}} = 26.8 \text{ m/s} \quad \textbf{(Units and standards)}$$

15. $65 \frac{\text{mi}}{\text{hr}} = 65 \frac{\text{mi}}{\text{hr}} \times \frac{1760 \text{ yds}}{1 \text{ mi}} \times \frac{3 \text{ ft}}{1 \text{ yd}} \times \frac{12 \text{ in}}{1 \text{ ft}} \times \left(\frac{2.54 \times 10^{-2} \text{ m}}{1 \text{ in}}\right)$

$$= 65 \times 1760 \times 3 \times 12 \times 2.54 \times 10^{-2} \text{ m/hr}$$

$$= 1.046 \times 10^5 \left(\frac{\text{m}}{\text{hr}}\right) \times \frac{1 \text{ km}}{1000 \text{ m}}$$

$$= \frac{1.046 \times 10^5}{1 \times 10^3} \frac{\text{km}}{\text{hr}} = 104.6 \text{ km/hr}$$

Similarly,

$55 \frac{\text{mi}}{\text{hr}} = 55 \times 1760 \times 3 \times 12 \times 2.54 \times 10^{-2}$ m/hr

$$= 8.851 \times 10^4 \text{ m/hr} = 8.851 \times 10^4 \frac{\text{m}}{\text{hr}}\left(\frac{1 \text{ km}}{1000 \text{ m}}\right)$$

$$= 88.5 \text{ km/hr}$$

Difference = 16.1 km/hr **(Units and standards)**

16. Weight of each block = 2.5 metric tons

Weight of 2 million blocks = $2.5 \times 2 \times 10^6$

$= 5 \times 10^6$ tons

Weight in lbs = 5×10^6 tons $\left(2205 \dfrac{\text{lbs}}{1 \text{ metric ton}}\right)$

$= 1.1 \times 10^{10}$ lbs

$= 11$ billion lbs   **(Units and standards)**

17. Price = \$1.35/gal = $\dfrac{\$1.35}{\text{gal}} \times \dfrac{1 \text{ gal}}{3.7853 \text{ liters}}$ = \$0.36/liter   **(Units and standards)**

18. One acre = 43,560 ft^2 = 43,560(1 ft × 1 ft)

$= 43560 \times (12 \times 2.54 \times 10^{-2} \text{ m})(12 \times 2.54 \times 10^{-2} \text{ m})$

$= 4.047 \times 10^3$ m^2

4,047 m^2 will fit in an acre of land.   **(Units and standards)**

19. 1 nanosecond = 1×10^{-9} s

Distance = $3 \times 10^8 \times 1 \times 10^{-9}$ m = 3×10^{-1} m = 30 cm   **(Units and standards)**

20. One foot = 12 in × $\dfrac{2.54 \times 10^{-2} \text{ m}}{1 \text{ in}}$ = 0.3048 m

100 cu. ft. = 100 × 1 cu. ft.

$= 100 \times (1 \text{ ft})^3$

$= 100 \times (0.3048 \text{ m})^3$

$= 2.83$ m^3 **(Units and standards)**

21. (a) 5 mm

    (b) 4 microsecond = 4 μs

    (c) 2 kg

    (d) 8 nanometer = 8 nm   **(Units and standards)**

22. Volume of cylinder = $V = \pi r^2 L$

$\sim (m)^2(m) \sim m^3$

Density = $\dfrac{\text{Mass}}{\text{Volume}} \Rightarrow \dfrac{\text{kg}}{\text{m}^3}$ **(Dimensional analysis)**

23. $x = at^2$

$a = \dfrac{x}{t^2} \sim \dfrac{m}{(s)^2} = m/s^2$ (**Dimensional analysis**)

24. $u^2 = u_0^2 + 2ax$

$2ax = u^2 - u_0^2$

$x = \dfrac{u^2 - u_0^2}{2a} = \dfrac{u^2}{2a} - \dfrac{u_0^2}{2a}$

Taking any one of the two terms on right side

$\dfrac{u_0^2}{2a} \sim \dfrac{(m/s)^2}{m/s^2} = \dfrac{m^2}{s^2}\left(\dfrac{s^2}{m}\right) = m$

So, meter is the unit of distance.   (**Dimensional analysis**)

25. The correct answer is (b). $\pi = 3.142$ (**Significant figures**)

26. The correct answer is (a). 4   (**Significant figures**)

27. Area = $41.22 \times 25.49 = 1050.6978$

Area = 1051 m^2 There are 4 significant figures in each length, and hence 4 in the product.

   (**Significant figures**)

28. Volume = $105 \text{ cm} \times 26.8 \text{ cm} \times 2.6 \text{ cm}$

$= 105 \times 26.8 \times 2.6 \text{ cm}^3$

$= 7316.4 \text{ cm}^3$

$= 7{,}300 \text{ cm}^3$

There are two significant figures in the height (2.6). As this is the measurement having the least number of significant figures, the answer also has this number of significant figures. (**Significant figures**)

29. Density of population = $\dfrac{119 \times 10^6}{55{,}000 \text{ sq. mi.}}$

$= 2.1636 \times 10^3 / \text{ sq. mi.}$

$= 2{,}200$ per sq. miles   (**Significant figures**)

30. Number of pages = $\dfrac{3.4 \text{ cm}}{5 \times 10^{-3} \text{ cm}} = 6.8 \times 10^2 = 680$

$= 700$ (**Significant figures**)

31. Volume = 5.2 × 3.925 × 2.25 m³

    = 45.9225 m³

    = 46 m³   (**Significant figures**)

32. 3.00×10⁸ m/s and 2.998×10⁸ m/s   (**Significant figures**)

33. Density = $\dfrac{55 \text{ g}}{2.85 \text{ cc}} = \dfrac{55}{2.85}\dfrac{\text{g}}{\text{cm}^3}\cdot\dfrac{1 \text{ kg}}{1000 \text{ g}}$

    Density = $\dfrac{55}{2.85 \times 1000}\dfrac{\text{kg}}{(1 \text{ cm})^3} = \dfrac{55 \text{ kg }(1 \text{ cm})^{-3}}{1000 \times 2.85}$

    $= \dfrac{55 \text{ kg}}{2.85 \times 10^3}\left[1 \text{ cm}\left(\dfrac{1 \text{ m}}{100 \text{ cm}}\right)\right]^{-3}$

    $= \dfrac{55 \text{ kg}}{2.85 \times 10^3}\left[\dfrac{1}{100}\text{ m}\right]^{-3} = \dfrac{55 \text{ kg}}{2.85 \times 10^3}[0.01 \text{ m}]^{-3}$

    $= \dfrac{55 \text{ kg}}{2.85 \times 10^3} \times [1 \times 10^{-2} \text{ m}]^{-3}$

    $= \dfrac{55 \text{ kg}}{2.85 \times 10^3} \times 10^6 \text{ m}^{-3}$

    = 1.9298×10⁴ kg/m³

    = 1.9×10⁴ kg/m³   (**Significant figures**)

34. Volume = 12 in × 18 in × 3 in

    = (12 × 2.54×10⁻² m) × (18 × 2.54×10⁻² m) × (3 × 2.54×10⁻² m)

    = 1.062×10⁻² m³ = 0.01 m³   (**Significant figures**)

35. Total Area = [(15 × 10) × 4 + 15 × 15] sq. ft.

    $= 825 \text{ (1 ft)}^2 = (825)\left[1 \text{ ft} \times \dfrac{12 \text{ in}}{1 \text{ ft}} \times \dfrac{2.54 \times 10^{-2} \text{ m}}{1 \text{ in}}\right]^2$

    = 825 × (3.048×10⁻¹ m)²

    = 825 × 9.29×10⁻² m²

    = 76.6 m²

    = 76.6 m²   (**Significant figures**)

36. Number of heartbeats = $75 \times 365 \times 24 \times 60 \times 70$

    $= 2.7594 \times 10^9$

    $= 2.8 \times 10^9$

    ≈ 3 billion times   **(Estimate/order of magnitude)**

37. Volume = $\pi r^2 L = \pi (3 \text{ cm})^2 (12 \text{ cm})$

    $= 339.3 \text{ cm}^3$

    $\approx 3 \times 10^2 \text{ cm}^3$ **(Estimate/order of magnitude)**

38. The correct answer is (b). The thickness of a dime = 1×10^{-3} m   **(Estimate/order of magnitude)**

39. The correct answer is (c). Number of minutes = $365 \times 24 \times 60 = 525,600 \approx 5.256 \times 10^5$

    (Estimate/order of magnitude)

40. Amount of toothpaste

    $= 170 \text{ g} \times 2 \times 12 \times 60 \times 10^6$

    $= 2448 \times 10^8 \text{ g}$

    $= 2.448 \times 10^8 \text{ kg}$

    $\approx 245 \times 10^6 \text{ kg}$

    = About 245 million kilograms

    Cost = $\$1.50 \times 2 \times 12 \times 60 \times 10^6$

    $= \$2.16 \times 10^9$

    ≈ 2 billion dollars   **(Estimate/order of magnitude)**

41. Amount = $450 \times 5 \times \dfrac{12,000}{3,000} \times 120 \times 10^6 \text{ g}$

    $= 1.08 \times 10^{12} \text{ g} = 1.08 \times 10^9 \text{ kg}$

    Amount ≈ 1 billion kg

    Cost = $\$1.20 \times 5 \times \dfrac{12,000}{3,000} \times 120 \times 10^6$

    $= \$2.88 \times 10^9$

    ≈ 3 billion dollars   **(Estimate/order of magnitude)**

Grade Yourself

Circle the question numbers that you had incorrect. Then indicate the number of questions you missed. If you answered more than three questions incorrectly, you need to focus on that topic. (If a topic has less than three questions and you had at least one wrong, we suggest you study that topic also. Read your textbook, a review book, or ask your teacher for help.)

Subject: Measurement and Analysis

Topic	Question Numbers	Number Incorrect
Measurement	1, 2, 3, 4, 5, 6, 7, 8, 9, 10	
Units and standards	11, 12, 13, 14, 15, 16, 17, 18, 19, 20, 21	
Dimensional analysis	22, 23, 24	
Significant figures	25, 26, 27, 28, 29, 30, 31, 32, 33, 34, 35	
Estimate/order of magnitude	36, 37, 38, 39, 40, 41	

Motion in One Dimension

 ## Brief Yourself

This is the study of objects moving in one dimension. In the study of motion, there are generally three quantities of interest. These are distance traveled (x), velocity (v), and acceleration (a) of the object undergoing motion. Most people are familiar with speed. Speed is equal to distance traveled per unit time. In physics, we introduce velocity, a quantity similar to speed. Speed has magnitude only. Velocity has magnitude and direction. It can be positive or negative depending on direction.

If we know the initial velocity (v_o) and the final velocity (v), the average velocity $<v>$ under constant acceleration is:

$$<v> = (v_o + v)/2 \qquad (1)$$

and the distance traveled by the object in time (t) is:

$$x = [(v_o + v)/2]t \qquad (2)$$

In this chapter, only constant acceleration is considered. An object may move at constant velocity or it may change its velocity during its motion. It is the presence of acceleration that changes the velocity of an object. In many problems, the final velocity is not given; instead, acceleration is stated. One may show that the final velocity is given by:

$$v = v_o + at \qquad (3)$$

When the above expression is combined with equation (2), we have:

$$x = v_o t + (1/2)at^2 \qquad (4)$$

One may solve for time (t) in equation (3) and substitute it in (4) to obtain a derived expression,

$$v^2 = v_o^2 + 2ax \qquad (5)$$

It is very important to be familiar with equations (3), (4), and (5). These three are all you need to solve any problem in one-dimensional motion.

In freely falling objects, the motion takes place in the presence of acceleration, due to gravity (g) in a vertical direction. Under this condition, you need only replace acceleration "a" by "g" in equations (3), (4), and (5).

Test Yourself

1. A space shuttle travels 25 miles in 5 seconds. What is its average speed in m/s?

2. An Amtrak train leaves the station from rest traveling 500 m in 3 minutes. Find the average velocity of the train in mph.

3. An athlete completes a 100 m run in 10.5 seconds. What is the average velocity in m/s?

4. Electrons strike a TV screen to trace out a picture. The speed of these electrons is 150,000,000 m/s over a distance of 35 cm. Find the time of travel.

5. You drive your car from home at a constant speed to a local shopping center 5 miles away in 10 minutes and come back in 10 minutes at the same constant speed. What is the velocity and the speed of your car in m/s averaged over the entire trip?

6. In a thunder storm, you hear the sound of the thunder 4 seconds after the lightning flash in the sky overhead. If the speed of sound in air is 340 m/s, how high are the clouds?

7. In a baseball game, the pitcher throws a fast ball with a horizontal speed of 98 mph toward the plate at 61 ft away. How long will the batter see the ball in the air before it arrives?

8. A sail boat crosses a river to an opposite point in 30 minutes moving at a uniform speed of 15 mph. It then moves back to the initial point at a uniform speed of 15 mph.

    (a) What is the width of the river in meters?
    (b) What is the net velocity during the trip forward and backward?

9. A leopard starting from rest runs 300 meters at a constant acceleration in 15 seconds to catch a deer. What is its instant velocity after 5 seconds?

10. A basketball player runs 10 m at a constant acceleration in 2.5 seconds moving straight ahead starting from rest. What is the instantaneous velocity of the player after 1 second?

11. While jogging on a straight sidewalk, you change your speed from 0.5 m/s to 0.98 m/s in 2 seconds. What is your uniform acceleration?

12. A jet plane achieves a speed of 500 mph in 10 minutes starting from an initial speed of 100 mph. What is its acceleration in m/s^2?

13. A train 500 m long passes a railroad crossing in 1 minute. If the initial velocity of the approaching train is 15 mph, what is the acceleration of the train?

14. You brought the car to a halt by applying the brake for 3 seconds. If the initial speed of your car was 50 mph, what was the deceleration of the car in m/s^2?

15. A bullet penetrates 7 cm into wood when fired at a speed of 33 m/s. Find the deceleration and the time taken to stop.

16. A tennis player moves in a straight line motion as shown in the distance versus time graph below. What is her velocity between points O and A?

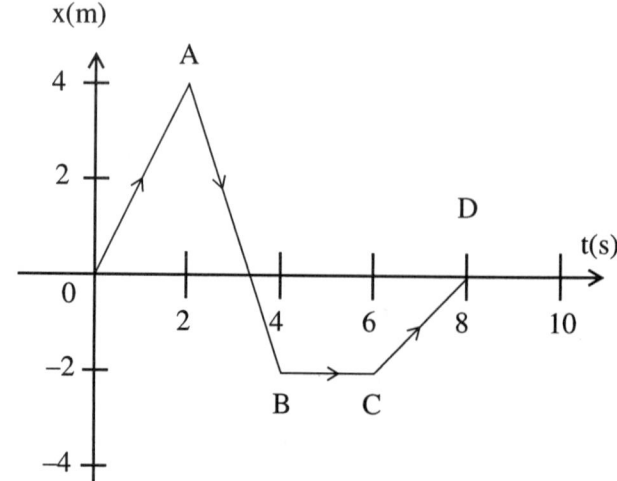

17. In the diagram of question number 16, what is the velocity between the points A an B?

18. In the diagram of question number 16, what is the velocity between the points B an C?

19. In the diagram of question number 16, what is the average velocity between the points between O and D?

20. A police car started chasing a speeding car on a straight highway. If the police car was accelerating at 2 m/s², starting from rest, what was its instant velocity in mph after 25 seconds?

21. The velocity versus time graph of a football player running in a straight line motion is shown below. What is the acceleration between points A and B?

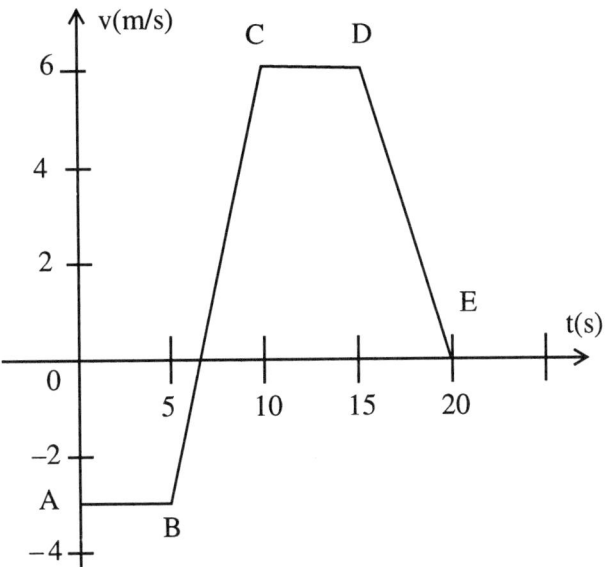

22. In the diagram of question number 21, what is the acceleration between points B and C?

23. In the diagram of question number 21, what is the acceleration between points D and E?

24. In order to pass the physical fitness examination, a cadet must run 2 miles in 20 minutes starting from rest. What is the uniform acceleration in m/s² needed to do the job?

25. A beach ball is thrown vertically upward from the ground with a speed of 15 m/s. Gravitational acceleration is 9.8 m/s² downward.
    (a) How high does it rise?
    (b) How long will it be airborne?
    (c) What is its velocity and acceleration at the highest point?

26. A boy drops a rock initially at rest from a bridge into the river below and watches it strike the water 3.5 seconds later. How high is the bridge over the water level?

27. A child drops a toy at rest from the window of a building 25 m above the ground.
    (a) How long will the toy be in the air before striking the ground?
    (b) What is the instantaneous velocity just before striking the ground?

28. What should the initial upward velocity of a ball be if it just reaches the roof of a house 50 m high?

29. A paratrooper descending at a constant speed of 5 m/s, accidentally drops his survival kit 200 m from the ground. How long after the kit will the paratrooper touch the ground?

30. The Columbia space shuttle accelerates upward at 30 m/s², starting from rest. How long will it take to achieve a vertical velocity of 2,500 mph?

31. A hot air balloon is descending at a constant speed of 10 mph. Unfortunately, the platform accidentally is separated from the balloon at a height of 150 ft. Find the final velocity in m/s of the platform just before hitting the ground.

32. A girl throws a stone vertically upward with an initial speed of 8 m/s from the ground.
    (a) How high will it rise?
    (b) How long will it take to return to the ground?

33. A homemade toy rocket accelerates vertically upward at 5 m/s², starting from rest on the ground. It runs out of fuel in 5 seconds.
    (a) How high from the ground will the rocket climb?
    (b) What is the time of flight of the rocket's complete journey?

34. A kingfisher dives vertically down from rest to catch a fish on the surface of a lake 30 m below. It catches the fish in 2 seconds.
    (a) What must its acceleration be?
    (b) What was its final velocity just before catching the prey?

16 / Physics I

Check Yourself

1. $25 \text{ mi} = 25 \times 1760 \times 3 \times 12 \times 2.54 \times 10^{-2} = 4.02 \times 10^4 \text{ m}$

   Average Speed $= \dfrac{4.02 \times 10^4 \text{ m}}{5 \text{ s}} = 8.04 \times 10^3$ m/s

   (Speed and velocity)

2. Average Velocity $= \dfrac{500 \text{ m}}{3 \text{ min}} = \dfrac{500 \text{ m}}{3 \text{ min}} \times \dfrac{1 \text{ km}}{1000 \text{ m}} \times \dfrac{60 \text{ min}}{1 \text{ hr}}$

   $= \dfrac{500 \times 1 \times 60}{3 \times 1000 \times 1} \dfrac{\text{km}}{\text{hr}} = 10$ km/hr

   1 km/hr = 0.6215 mi/hr

   Average Velocity = 10×0.6215 mi/hr = 6.2 mph

   (Speed and velocity)

3. Average Velocity $= \dfrac{100 \text{ m}}{10.5 \text{ s}} = 9.52$ m/s

   (Speed and velocity)

4. $35 \text{ cm} = 35 \text{ cm} \times \dfrac{1 \text{ m}}{100 \text{ cm}} = 0.35 \text{ m}$

   $v = \dfrac{x}{t}$

   $t = \dfrac{x}{v} = \dfrac{0.35 \text{ m}}{150{,}000{,}000 \text{ m/s}} = 2.33 \times 10^{-9}$ s

   Time, t = 2.33 nanoseconds (We are ignoring corrections for relativity.)

   (Speed and velocity)

5. Average Velocity $= \dfrac{v_0 + v}{2} = \dfrac{v - v}{t} = \dfrac{0}{t} = 0$

   Average Speed $= \dfrac{10 \text{ mi}}{20 \text{ min}} = \dfrac{10 \text{ mi}}{20 \text{ min}} \times \dfrac{60 \text{ min}}{1 \text{ hr}}$

   $= \dfrac{10 \times 60}{20}$ mi/hr = 30 mi/hr

   1 mi/hr $= \dfrac{1 \times 1760 \times 3 \times 12 \times 2.54 \times 10^{-2} \text{ m}}{60 \times 60 \text{ s}}$

   $= 0.447$ m/s

Average Speed = $30 \times 0.447 = 13.4$ m/s

(Speed and velocity)

6. $v = \dfrac{x}{t}$, $x = vt = 340 \times 4 = 1{,}360$ m

   1,360 m high. **(Speed and velocity)**

7. $v = \dfrac{x}{t}$, $t = \dfrac{x}{v} = \dfrac{61 \text{ ft}}{98 \text{ mi/hr}}$

   $t = \dfrac{61 \text{ ft} \times \text{hr}}{98 \text{ mi}} = \dfrac{61 \text{ ft} \times \text{hr}}{98 \text{ mi}} \times \dfrac{1 \text{ mi}}{1760 \times 3 \text{ ft}}$

   $= \dfrac{61 \times 1}{98 \times 1760 \times 3} \text{ hr}$

   $= \dfrac{61 \times 60 \times 60 \text{ s}}{98 \times 1760 \times 3} = 0.42$ s

   (Speed and velocity)

8. (a) $v = \dfrac{x}{t}$

   $x = vt = \left(15 \dfrac{\text{mi}}{\text{hr}}\right)(30 \text{ min})$

   $= \dfrac{15 \times 30}{\text{hr}} (\text{mi})(\text{min}) = \dfrac{15 \times 30 (\text{mi})(\text{min})}{1 \text{ hr}} \dfrac{(1 \text{ hr})}{60 \text{ min}}$

   $= \dfrac{15 \times 30 \text{ mi}}{60} = 7.5$ mi

   $x = 7.5 \times 1.609 \times 10^3 = 1.21 \times 10^4$ m

   (b) $v = \dfrac{v_0 + v}{2} = \dfrac{v - v}{2} = \dfrac{0}{2} = 0$

   (Speed and velocity)

9. $x = v_0 t + \dfrac{1}{2} a t^2$

   $300 = 0 + \dfrac{1}{2}(a)(15)^2 = \dfrac{225}{2} a$

   $a = \dfrac{300 \times 2}{225} = 2.67$ m/s^2

   $v = v_0 + at$

   $v = 0 + 2.67 \times 5 = 13.3$ m/s **(Instantaneous velocity)**

10. $$x = v_0 t + \frac{1}{2}at^2 = 0 + \frac{1}{2}(a)t^2$$

$$10 = \frac{1}{2}a(2.5)^2 = \frac{6.25a}{2}$$

$$a = \frac{10 \times 2}{6.25} = 3.2 \text{ m/s}^2$$

$$v = v_0 + at$$

$$v = 0 + 3.2 \times 1$$

$$v = 3.2 \text{ m/s}$$

(Instantaneous velocity)

11. $$v = v_0 + at$$

$$0.98 = 0.5 + a(2)$$

$$2a = 0.98 - 0.5 = 0.48$$

$$a = 0.24 \text{ m/s}^2$$

(Constant acceleration)

12. $$1 \text{ mph} = 0.447 \text{ m/s}$$

$$10 \text{ min} = 10 \times 60 \text{ s} = 600 \text{ s}$$

$$v = v_0 + at$$

$$500(0.447) = 100 \times 0.447 + (a)600$$

$$600a = (500 - 100)0.447 = 400 \times 0.447$$

$$a = \frac{400 \times 0.447}{600} = 0.298 \text{ m/s}^2$$

(Constant acceleration)

13. $$x = v_0 t + \frac{1}{2}at^2$$

$$500 = (15 \times 0.447)(1 \times 60) + \frac{1}{2}(a)(1 \times 60)^2$$

$$500 = 402.3 + 1.8 \times 10^3 (a)$$

$$a = 5.43 \times 10^{-2} \text{ m/s}^2$$

(Constant acceleration)

14. $v = v_0 + at$

    $0 = (50 \times 0.447) + (a)3$

    $3a = -50 \times 0.447$

    $a = -\dfrac{50 \times 0.447}{3} = -7.45 \text{ m/s}^2$

    (Constant acceleration)

15. $v^2 = v_0^2 + 2ax$

    $0 = 33^2 + 2(a)(7 \times 10^{-2})$

    $a = -\dfrac{33 \times 33}{2 \times 7 \times 10^{-2}} = -7.78 \times 10^3 \text{ m/s}^2$

    $v = v_0 + at$

    $0 = 33 - (7.78 \times 10^3)t$

    $t = \dfrac{33}{7.78 \times 10^3} = 4.24 \times 10^{-3} \text{ s}$

    $t = 4.24$ milliseconds

    (Constant acceleration)

16.

    OA: $v = \dfrac{x_2 - x_1}{t} = \dfrac{4}{2} = 2$ m/s **(Speed and velocity)**

20 / Physics I

17. AB: $v = \dfrac{x_2 - x_1}{t} = \dfrac{-2-4}{2} = \dfrac{-6}{2} = -3$ m/s (Speed and velocity)

18. BC: $v = \dfrac{x_2 - x_1}{t} = \dfrac{-2+2}{2} = 0$ (Speed and velocity)

19. OD: $v = \dfrac{x_2 - x_1}{t} = \dfrac{0}{t} = 0$ (Speed and velocity)

20. $v = v_0 + at$

    $v = 0 + 2(25)$

    $v = 50$ m/s

    $v = \dfrac{50}{0.447} = 111.8$ mi/hr

    (Instantaneous velocity)

21.

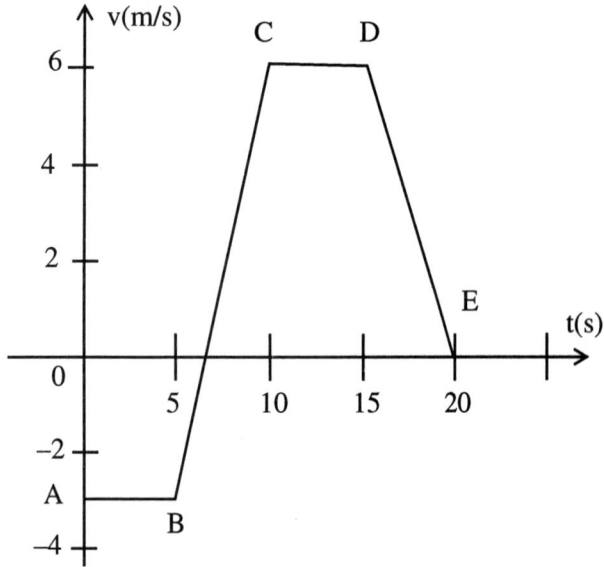

AB: $a = \dfrac{v_2 - v_1}{t} = \dfrac{-3+3}{5} = \dfrac{0}{5} = 0$

(Constant acceleration)

22. BC: $a = \dfrac{v_2 - v_1}{t} = \dfrac{6+3}{5} = \dfrac{9}{5} = 1.8$ m/s^2

(Constant acceleration)

23. DE: $a = \dfrac{v_2 - v_1}{t} = \dfrac{0-6}{5} = \dfrac{-6}{5} = -1.2 \text{ m/s}^2$

    (Constant acceleration)

24. $x = v_0 t + \dfrac{1}{2} a t^2$

    $(2 \times 1{,}760 \times 3 \times 12 \times 2.54 \times 10^{-2}) \text{m} = 0 + \dfrac{1}{2}(a)(20 \times 60 \text{ s})^2$

    $a = \dfrac{2 \times 1609.3}{(20 \times 60)^2} \text{ m/s}^2$

    $a = 2.2 \times 10^{-3} \text{ m/s}^2$

    (Constant acceleration)

25. (a) $v_0 = 15$ m/s

    $a = g = -9.8 \text{ m/s}^2$

    $v = 0$ at the top of the ball's rise

    $v^2 = v_0^2 + 2ay$

    $0 = 15^2 - 2 \times 9.8 \times y$

    $y = \dfrac{15^2}{2 \times 9.8} = 11.5 \text{ m}$

    (b) $v = v_0 + gt$, considering the time to the top of the ball's rise we have,

    $0 = 15 - 9.8 t_1$

    $t_1 = \dfrac{15}{9.8} = 1.53$

    Round trip $= 2 t_1 = 3.06$ s

    (c) $v = 0$

    $a = g = -9.8 \text{ m/s}^2 = $ constant

    (Free fall)

26. $y = v_0 t + \dfrac{1}{2} a t^2$

    $y = 0 + \dfrac{1}{2}(-9.8)(3.5)^2 = -60 \text{ m}$

The bridge is 60 m high.

(Free fall)

27. (a) $y = v_0 t + \frac{1}{2} a t^2$

    $-25 = 0 + \frac{1}{2}(-9.8)t^2$

    $t^2 = \frac{50}{9.8}, t = 2.26$ s

    (b) $v = v_0 + at$

    $v = 0 - 9.8(2.26)$

    $v = -22.1$ m/s

    22.1 m/s downward

(Free fall)

28. $v^2 = v_0^2 + 2ay$

    At the top of the rise, $v = 0$

    $0 = v_0^2 + 2(-9.8)50$

    $v_0^2 = 980$

    $v_0 = 31.3$ m/s

(Free fall)

29. Let the descent of the paratrooper take time t_1.

    $v = \frac{y}{t}, t_1 = \frac{y}{v} = \frac{200}{5} = 40$ s

    Let the survival kit take time t_2.

    $y = v_0 t + \frac{1}{2} a t^2$

    $-200 = -5t + \frac{1}{2}(-9.8)t^2 = -5t - 4.9t^2$ (Note $v_o = -5$ because the paratrooper was already moving downward)

    $4.9t^2 + 5t - 200 = 0$

$$t = \frac{-b \pm \sqrt{b^2 - 4ac}}{2a} = \frac{5}{9.8} \pm \frac{(25 + 3920)^{\frac{1}{2}}}{9.8}$$

$$t_2 = \frac{-5 \pm 62.8}{9.8} = -6.9 \text{ s or } 5.9 \text{ s}$$

Time difference $= t_1 - t_2 = 40 - 5.9 = 34.1$ s

(Free fall)

30. 2,500 mph $= 2,500 \times 0.447$ m/s $= 1117.5$ m/s

$$v = v_0 + at$$

$$1117.5 = 0 + \frac{1}{2}(30)t^2$$

$$t = 37.2 \text{ s}$$

(Constant acceleration)

31. 10 mph $= 4.47$ m/s

150 ft $= 150 \times 12 \times 2.54 \times 10^{-2}$ m $= 45.7$ m

$$v^2 = v_0^2 + 2ay$$

$$v^2 = (4.47)^2 + 2(-9.8)(-45.7)$$

$$v^2 = 19.98 + 895.7 = 915.7$$

$$v = \pm 30.3 \text{ m/s}$$

$$v = -30.3 \text{ m/s}$$

(Free fall)

32. (a) $v^2 = v_0^2 + 2ay$

$$0 = 8^2 + 2(-9.8)y$$

$$19.6y = 64$$

$$y = \frac{64}{19.6} = 3.3 \text{ m}$$

(b) $v = v_0 + at$

$$0 = 8 + (-9.8)t$$

$t = \dfrac{8}{9.8} = 0.82$ s, total time $2t = 1.64$ s

(Free fall)

33.

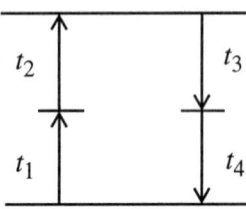

(a) The velocity at the point the fuel runs out is calculated from $v = v_0 + at$

$v_1 = v_0 + at_1$

$v_1 = 0 + 5(5)$

$v_1 = 25$ m/s

During this time, the rocket rises $y_1 = v_0 t_1 + \dfrac{1}{2}at_1^2 = 0 + \dfrac{1}{2}(5)5^2 = \dfrac{125}{2}$

$y_1 = 62.5$ m

After the fuel runs out, the rocket continues to rise until $v_2 = 0$. During that time, the additional rise is calculated from

$v_2^2 = v_1^2 + 2ay_2$

$0 = 25^2 + 2(-9.8)y_2$

$y_2 = \dfrac{625}{19.6} = 31.9$ m, The total rise is then $y = y_1 + y_2 = 94.4$ m

(b) To find t_2 $v = v_0 + at$

$v_2 = v_1 + (-9.8)t_2$

$0 = 25 - 9.8 t_2$

$t_2 = 2.5$ s, by reversing this last calculation for journey downward, we see $t_3 = 2.5$ s

$y = v_0 t + \dfrac{1}{2}at^2$

Finally, for t_4 we use

$$y_4 = v_4 t + \frac{1}{2}at^2$$

$$-y_1 = -v_1 t + \frac{1}{2}(-9.8)t^2$$

$$-62.5 = -25t - 4.9t^2$$

$$4.9t^2 + 25t - 62.5 = 0$$

$$t = \frac{-25}{9.8} \pm \frac{(625 + 1225)^{\frac{1}{2}}}{9.8} = -2.55 \pm 4.39$$

$$t_4 = 1.84 \text{ s}$$

$$T = t_1 + t_2 + t_3 + t_4 = 11.8 \text{ s}$$

(Free fall)

34. (a) $y = v_0 t + \frac{1}{2}at^2$

    $-30 = 0 + \frac{1}{2}(a)2^2$

    $a = \frac{-30}{2} = -15 \text{ m/s}^2$, 15 m/s^2 downward

    (b) $v = v_0 + at$

    $v = 0 - 15 \times 2$

    $v = -30$ m/s, 30 m/s downward

    (Constant acceleration)

Grade Yourself

Circle the question numbers that you had incorrect. Then indicate the number of questions you missed. If you answered more than three questions incorrectly, you need to focus on that topic. (If a topic has less than three questions and you had at least one wrong, we suggest you study that topic also. Read your textbook, a review book, or ask your teacher for help.)

Subject: Motion in One Dimension

Topic	Question Numbers	Number Incorrect
Speed and velocity	1, 2, 3, 4, 5, 6, 7, 8, 16, 17, 18, 19	
Instantaneous velocity	9, 10, 20	
Constant acceleration	11, 12, 13, 14, 15, 21, 22, 23, 24, 30, 34	
Free fall	25, 26, 27, 28, 29, 31, 32, 33	

Vectors

Brief Yourself

All physical quantities are divided into two groups, namely vectors and scalars. A scalar is a quantity that has magnitudes only. Examples are time, energy, speed, and distance. A vector is a quantity that has both magnitude and direction. Examples are velocity, acceleration, force, and momentum. Earlier, in Chapter 2, we introduced velocity. Another vector quantity of interest is *displacement*. The magnitude of the displacement is the straight line distance between two points. The direction of displacement is determined by a line joining the initial point to the final point.

In the Parallelogram Rule of Vector Addition, the two vectors being summed form the two adjacent arms of a parallelogram and the diagonal of this parallelogram becomes the resultant vector. When many vectors are joined together head to tail, as in a polygon, the resultant vector is the last remaining side of the polygon.

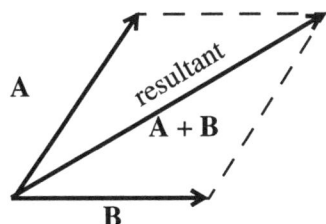

Parallelogram Rule of
Vector Addition

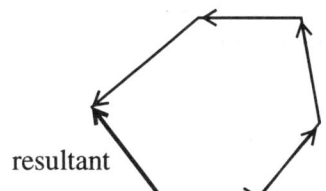

Polygon method

In the resolution of vectors, also called the component method of vector resolution, any vector in a two dimensional plane can be resolved into two perpendicular components along the *x* and *y* axes. Vectors do not add or subtract like ordinary numbers. This is because vectors have direction. Needless to say, there are no ordinary rules for summing directions. Whenever many vectors are added, the *x* component of the resultant vector is the sum of the *x* components and the *y* component of the resultant vector is the sum of the *y* components.

Vector **A** can be written as,

$\mathbf{A} = A_x\mathbf{i} + A_y\mathbf{j}$, where, $\mathbf{i}$ = unit vector along *x*-axis and $\mathbf{j}$ = unit vector along *y*-axis.

$A_x = A \cos \theta$ and, $A_y = A \sin \theta$, where θ is the angle A makes with the *x*-axis.

Also, the magnitude of vector **A** is,

$$A = [A_x^2 + A_y^2]^{1/2} \quad \text{and} \quad \frac{A_y}{A_x} = \tan\theta, \quad \text{so} \quad \theta = \tan^{-1}\left(\frac{A_y}{A_x}\right)$$

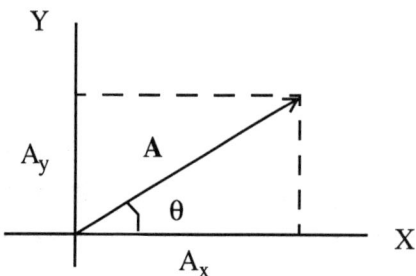

Two or more vectors can be added to find their resultant vector **R** as follows:

If **A** + **B** = **R**

then, $A_x + B_x = R_x$ and $A_y + B_y = R_y$

 ## Test Yourself

1. Bob walks 4 m north, turns right and walks 3 m east. What is the magnitude of Bob's displacement?

2. You are facing the side wall of a room which forms the x-y plane with its origin at the bottom left corner. The x and y coordinates of a tiny bug at rest on the wall are 5 m and 3 m, respectively. What are the polar coordinates (r, θ) of the bug?

3. Two forces acting on a body produce two instantaneous velocities on the same body at right angles. The resultant velocity of the body is 12 m/s at 30° to the x-axis. Find the magnitude of the two instantaneous velocities.

4. The coordinates of initial point A and final point B in the x-y plane are (2, 3) and (−1, 5) in meters. Find the displacement in magnitude and direction.

5. The polar coordinates of a point are 7 m and 125°. What are the x and y components?

6. If you walk 78 m north, make a U-turn and walk 30 m south, what is your displacement?

7. A jogger runs 150 m in a straight line on level ground and then climbs an inclined plane at 30° with the horizontal for 250 m straight ahead. What is the resultant displacement of the jogger?

8. A cat in search of prey runs 5 m north, then 2.5 m at an angle of 35° south of east, and finally 3 m east. Find the cat's resultant displacement vector.

9. A diver plunges into a lake moving 12 m at an angle of 45° with the horizontal, then moves 5 m vertically down and finally moves 8 m upward at an angle of 30° with the horizontal. How far below the surface of the lake is the diver?

10. The magnitude and direction of a vector are stated as 25 units at 37° from the horizontal. What are the x and y components of this vector?

11. A vector is represented by 175 units at 210° in a plane. Find its components.

12. The *x* and *y* components of a velocity are 11 m/s and 17 m/s, respectively. Find the magnitude and direction of this velocity.

13. What is the magnitude and direction of the velocity **V** if V_x = 3.5 m/s and V_y = –5.5 m/s?

14. The x and y components of two vectors **F**$_1$ and **F**$_2$ are (6, 9) and (5, 3), respectively. Find the resultant vector in magnitude and direction.

15. Three vectors with *x*, *y* components **A**(4, 7), **B**(3, 5), and **C**(2, 7) are combined to give **R**. Find the magnitude and direction of **R**.

16. Find the resultant displacement **D** of the three displacements given by **D**$_1$(7 m, 30°), **D**$_2$(9 m, 125°), and **D**$_3$(5 m, –45°).

17. Find sum **C** of two vectors **A** and **B** given by A_x = 4, A_y = 8, B_x = 3, and B_y = –7.

18. Find difference vector **D** of the two vectors **A** and **B** given by A_x = 2, A_y = –5, B_x = 4, and B_y = 7.

    D = A – B

19. The components of two vectors are A_x = 9, A_y = 6, B_x = 2, and B_y = –3. Find the *x* and *y* components of the resultant vector **R**, where

    R = 3A – 2B

20. The components of the two vectors are A_x = –6, A_y = 3, B_x = –2, and B_y = –5. Find the magnitude and direction of the resultant vector **R** where

    R = 3A – 2B

Check Yourself

1.

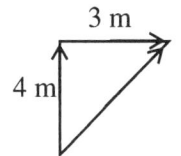

$$\text{Displacement} = \sqrt{4^2 + 3^2} = \sqrt{16 + 9} = \pm 5$$

Displacement = 5 m

(Vector addition)

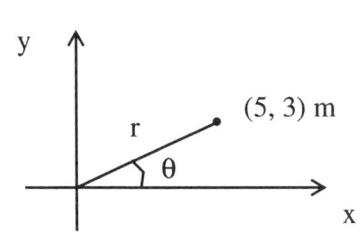

2.

$$r = \sqrt{x^2 + y^2} = \sqrt{5^2 + 3^2} = \sqrt{34} = \pm 5.83$$

$$\theta = \tan^{-1}\frac{y}{x} = \tan^{-1}\frac{3}{5} = 31°$$

$(r, \theta) = (5.8, 31°)$

(Coordinate system)

3. $x = r \cos\theta, y = r \sin\theta$

    $v_1 = v \cos\theta = 12 \cos 30° = 10.4$ m/s

    $v_2 = v \sin\theta = 12 \sin 30° = 6$ m/s

(Vector resolution)

4.

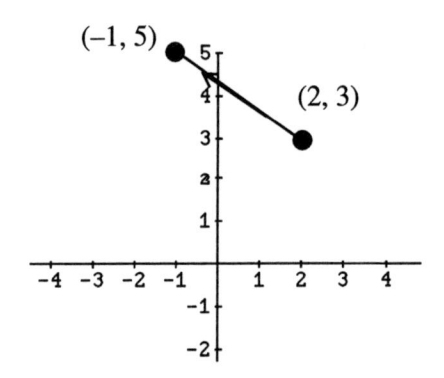

Magnitude of displacement,

$$D_{BA} = \sqrt{x^2 + y^2} = [(x_f - x_i)^2 + (y_f - y_i)^2]^{\frac{1}{2}}$$

$$= [(-1-2)^2 + (5-3)^2]^{\frac{1}{2}} = \sqrt{3^2 + 2^2} = \sqrt{13} = 3.6 \text{ m}$$

Direction, $\theta = \tan^{-1}\left(\dfrac{y}{x}\right)$

$\theta = \tan^{-1}\left[\dfrac{y_f - y_i}{x_f - x_i}\right] = \tan^{-1}\left(\dfrac{5-3}{-1-2}\right) = \tan^{-1}\left(\dfrac{2}{-3}\right)$

$\theta = 146.3°$

(Coordinate system)

5. $r = 7$ m, $\theta = 125°$

    $x = r \cos\theta = 7 \cos 125° = -4.01$

    $y = r \sin\theta = 7 \sin 125° = 5.73$

(Coordinate system)

6.

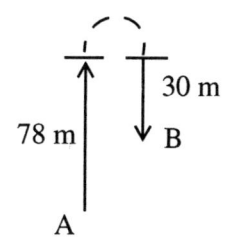

```
        ⌢
    ↑   ↓ 30 m
78 m    B
    ↑
    A
```

Here, A = (0, 0), B = (0, 48)

Magnitude = (48 – 0) = 48 m

Direction is north.

Displacement is 48 m north.

(Vector addition)

7.

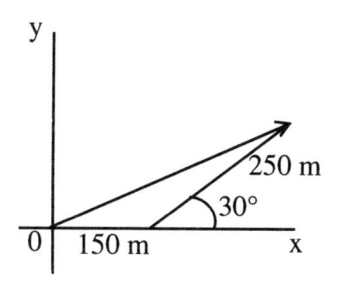

```
y
|       250 m ↗
|      30°
0  150 m      x
```

$D = D_1 + D_2$, $D_1 = (x_1, y_1) = (150 \text{ m}, 0)$

$D_2 = (x_2, y_2)$, $D = [(x_1 + x_2), (y_1 + y_2)]$

$x_2 = r\cos\theta = 250 \cos 30° = 216.5$

$y_2 = r\sin\theta = 250 \sin 30° = 125$

$x_1 + x_2 = 150 + 216.5 = 366.5$

$y_1 + y_2 = 0 + 125 = 125$

$D = (366.5 \text{ m}, 125 \text{ m})$

$D = [366.5^2 + 125^2]^{\frac{1}{2}} = (1.5 \times 10^5)^{\frac{1}{2}}$

$= 387.2 \text{ m}$

$\theta = \tan^{-1}\left(\frac{y}{x}\right) = \tan^{-1}\left[\frac{125}{366.5}\right] = 18.8°$

Displacement is 387.2 m at 18.8°.

(Vector addition)

8.

$D = D_1 + D_2 + D_3$

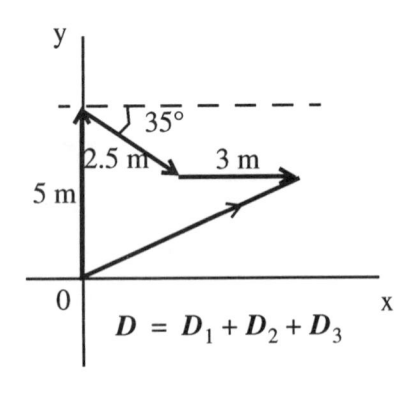

$D_1 = (x_1, y_1)$, $x_1 = 0$, $y_1 = 5$

$D_2 = (x_2, y_2)$

$x_2 = r\cos\theta = 2.5 \cos(-35°) = 2.05$

$y_2 = r\sin\theta = 2.5 \sin(-35°) = -1.43$

$D_3 = (x_3, y_3)$

$x_3 = r\cos\theta = 3 \cos 0° = 3$, $y_3 = r\sin\theta = 3 \sin 0° = 0$

$D = (x, y)$

$x = x_1 + x_2 + x_3 = 0 + 2.05 + 3 = 5.05$

$y = y_1 + y_2 + y_3 = 5 - 1.43 + 0 = 3.57$

$x^2 + y^2 = 5.05^2 + 3.57^2 = 38.2$

$D = \sqrt{x^2 + y^2} = 6.2$ m

$\theta = \tan^{-1}\left(\dfrac{y}{x}\right) = \tan^{-1}\left(\dfrac{3.57}{5.05}\right) = 35.3°$

Displacement is 6.2 m at 35.3°.

(Vector addition)

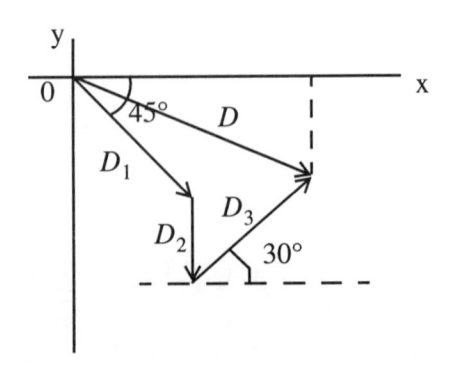

9.

$D = D_1 + D_2 + D_3$

$D_1 = (x_1, y_1)$, $x_1 = r\cos\theta = 12\cos(-45°) = 8.48$

$y_1 = 12\sin(-45°) = -8.48$

$D_2 = (x_2, y_2)$, $x_2 = 0$, $y_2 = -5$

$D_3 = (x_3, y_3)$

$x_3 = 8\cos 30° = 6.93$

$y_3 = 8\sin 30 = 4$

$D = (x, y)$

$x = x_1 + x_2 + x_3 = 8.48 + 0 + 6.93 = 15.4$

$y = y_1 + y_2 + y_3 = -8.48 + (-5) + 4 = -9.48$

So, the diver is 9.5 m below the surface of the lake.

(Vector addition)

10. $A = (25, 37°)$

    $x = 25\cos 37° = 20.0$

    $y = 25\sin 37° = 15.0$

    (Vector resolution)

11. $A = (175, 210°)$

    $x = 175\cos 210° = -151.5$

    $y = 175\sin 210° = -87.5$

    (Coordinate system)

12. $\sqrt{11^2 + 17^2} = \sqrt{410} = 20.2$

    $\theta = \tan^{-1}\left(\dfrac{y}{x}\right) = \tan^{-1}\left(\dfrac{17}{11}\right) = 57.1°$

    Velocity is 20.2 m/s at 57.1°.

    (Vector resolution)

13. $v = \sqrt{v_x^2 + v_y^2} = \sqrt{3.5^2 + (-5.5)^2}$

    $v = 6.52$

$$\theta = \tan^{-1}\left(\frac{v_y}{v_x}\right) = \tan^{-1}\left(\frac{-5.5}{3.5}\right) = -57.5°$$

$\theta = -57.5°$ or $122.5°$

Velocity is 6.5 m/s at $-57.5°$ (4th quadrant).

(Vector resolution)

14. $F_1 = (x_1, y_1) = (6, 9)$

    $F_2 = (x_2, y_2) = (5, 3)$

    $F = F_1 + F_2$

    $F = x, y, \; x = x_1 + x_2 = 6 + 5 = 11$

    $y = y_1 + y = 9 + 3 = 12$

    $F = \sqrt{11^2 + 12^2} = \sqrt{265} = 16.3$

    $\theta = \tan^{-1}\left(\frac{y}{x}\right) = \tan^{-1}\left(\frac{12}{11}\right) = 47.5°$

    Resultant vector is 16.3 at 47.5°.

    (Vector addition)

15. $R = A + B + C$

    $A = (x_1, y_1) = (4, 7)$

    $B = (x_2, y_2) = (3, 5)$

    $C = (x_3, y_3) = (2, 7)$

    $R = (x, y)$

    $x = x_1 + x_2 + x_3 = 4 + 3 + 2 = 9$

    $y = y_1 + y_2 + y_3 = 7 + 5 + 7 = 19$

    $R = \sqrt{x^2 + y^2} = \sqrt{9^2 + 19^2} = \sqrt{442} = 21$

    $\theta = \tan^{-1}\left(\frac{y}{x}\right) = \tan^{-1}\left(\frac{19}{9}\right) = 64.6°$

    Resultant vector is 21 units at 64.6°.

    (Vector addition)

16. $D = D_1 + D_2 + D_3$

$D_1 = (x_1, y_1)$, $x_1 = r\cos\theta = 7\cos 30° = 6.06$

$y_1 = r\sin\theta = 7\sin 30° = 3.5$

$D_2 = (x_2, y_2)$, $x_2 = 9\cos 125° = -5.16$

$y_2 = 9\sin 125° = 7.37$

$D_3 = (x_3, y_3)$, $x_3 = 5\cos(-45°) = 3.53$

$y_3 = 5\sin(-45°) = -3.53$

$D = (x, y)$

$x = x_1 + x_2 + x_3 = 6.06 + (-5.16) + 3.53$

$x = 4.43$

$y = y_1 + y_2 + y_3 = 3.5 + 7.37 + (-3.53)$

$y = 7.34$

$D = \sqrt{x^2 + y^2} = \sqrt{4.43^2 + 7.34^2} = \sqrt{73.50}$

$D = 8.57$

$\theta = \tan^{-1}\left(\frac{y}{x}\right) = \tan^{-1}\left(\frac{7.34}{4.43}\right) = 58.9°$

Resultant displacement is 8.7 m at 58.9°.

(Vector resolution)

17. $C = (x, y)$

$x = A_x + B_x = 4 + 3 = 7$

$y = A_y + B_y = 8 - 7 = 1$

$C_x = 7$

$C_y = 1$

$C = 7i + j$ where i is the unit vector in the x direction and j is the unit vector in the y direction.

(Vector addition)

18. $D = A - B$

   $D_x = A_x - B_x = (2-4) = -2$

   $D_y = A_y - B_y = (-5-7) = -12$

   $D = -2i - 12j$

   (Vector addition)

19. $R = 3A - 2B$

   $R_x = 3A_x - 2B_x = 3(9) - 2(2) = 27 - 4 = 23$

   $R_y = 3A_y - 2B_y = 3(6) - 2(-3) = 18 + 6 = 12$

   $R = 23i + 12j$

   (Vector addition)

20. $R = 3A - 2B$

   $R_x = 3A_x - 2B_x = 3(-6) - 2(-2) = -18 + 4 = -14$

   $R_y = 3A_y - 2B_y = 3(3) - 2(-5) = 9 + 10 = 19$

   $R = [(-14)^2 + 19^2]^{1/2} = \sqrt{557} = 23.6$

   $\theta = \tan^{-1}\left(\dfrac{19}{-14}\right) = -53.6° \text{ or } 126.4°$

   Resultant vector is 23.6 units at 126.4°.

   (Vector addition)

Grade Yourself

Circle the question numbers that you had incorrect. Then indicate the number of questions you missed. If you answered more than three questions incorrectly, you need to focus on that topic. (If a topic has less than three questions and you had at least one wrong, we suggest you study that topic also. Read your textbook, a review book, or ask your teacher for help.)

Subject: Vectors

Topic	Question Numbers	Number Incorrect
Vector addition	1, 6, 7, 8, 9, 14, 15, 17, 18, 19, 20	
Coordinate system	2, 4, 5, 11	
Vector resolution	3, 10, 12, 13, 16	

Motion in Two Dimensions

4

Brief Yourself

This is the study of objects moving in a plane. In many ways, the equations you have learned in one dimensional motion in Chapter 2 can now be extended to two dimensions. The equations for motion in a plane can now be written as:

$$v_x = v_{ox} + a_x t \tag{1}$$

$$v_y = v_{oy} + a_y t \tag{2}$$

where the subscript o stands for original or initial velocity. Subscripts x and y stand for the x and y components of the velocity.

The displacement in two dimensional motion may be written as:

$$x = v_{ox} t + (1/2) a_x t^2 \tag{3}$$

$$y = v_{oy} t + (1/2) a_y t^2 \tag{4}$$

and,

$$v_x^2 = v_{ox}^2 + 2 a_x x \tag{5}$$

$$v_y^2 = v_{oy}^2 + 2 a_y y \tag{6}$$

When studying the motion of an object in a vertical plane under the influence of gravity, it is known as projectile motion. In this situation, there is no acceleration in the horizontal direction along the x-axis ($a_x = 0$). However, the presence of vertical acceleration downward is due to gravity and $a_y = -g$. The equations of motion for a projectile may be written as:

$$v_x = v_{ox} = \text{Constant} \tag{7}$$

$$v_y = v_{oy} - gt \tag{8}$$

$$x = v_{ox} t \tag{9}$$

$$y = v_{oy} t - (1/2) g t^2 \tag{10}$$

$$v_y^2 = v_{oy}^2 - 2gy \tag{11}$$

The path taken by a projectile under the influence of gravity is parabolic. In polar coordinates:

$$v_x = v_o \cos\theta_o = \text{Constant} \tag{12}$$

$$v_y = v_o \sin\theta_o - gt \tag{13}$$

$$x = v_o \cos\theta_o t \tag{14}$$

$$y = v_{oy} t - (1/2)gt^2 \tag{15}$$

$$v_y^2 = v_{oy}^2 - 2gy \tag{16}$$

Here θ_o is the initial angle of throwing the projectile with respect to the horizontal. The range R of a projectile is:

$$R = \left[\frac{v_o^2}{g}\right] \sin 2\theta_o \tag{15}$$

In many situations, navigators, engineers, and physicists face the problem of relative motion. The frame of reference on the ground is usually considered to be a fixed frame of reference named S. Sometimes, motion of objects takes place in buses, trains, planes, air (current), or water (current), which are in motion. The frame of reference which is fixed in the moving bodies or media (but otherwise moving at constant velocity with respect to S) is usually named as S'. Unprimed symbols r (position), v (velocity), and a (acceleration) are used to refer to physical quantities of the object relative to the fixed frame of reference on the ground. Similarly, primed symbols such as r', v', and a' are the physical quantities of the same object with respect to the moving frame S'. Simple rules, as in addition of vectors, apply for determining the relative motion of objects.

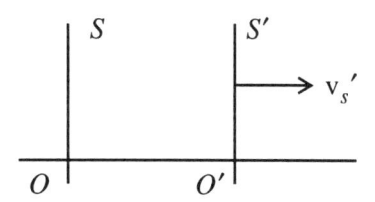

$$\mathbf{r} = \mathbf{r}_s' + \mathbf{r}'$$

$$\mathbf{v} = \mathbf{v}_s' + \mathbf{v}'$$

$$\mathbf{a} = \mathbf{a}'$$

The subscript s refers to the motion of O' with respect to O. The above equations show how a description of motion in one frame of reference may be related to the description of motion in another frame of reference. The equations are sometimes referred to as transformation equations.

Test Yourself

1. A rock is thrown from the ground at a speed of 22 m/s and an angle of 55° above the horizontal. Find the velocity and height of the rock after 2s.

2. A bullet is fired horizontally with a speed of 500 m/s from a height of 1.5 m above the ground toward a target 50 m away on the ground. How high should the target be placed to receive the bullet?

3. A boat moves north at a uniform velocity of 15 mph relative to the shore from one side of the river to a point directly opposite on the other side of the river. The water in the river flows east at a constant speed of 5 mph parallel to the shore. What is the velocity of the boat relative to the water?

4. A ship travels north at 6 m/s. The wind travels west at 2.5 m/s. In what direction will the pennant of the ship on the masthead fly?

5. A player kicks a football from the ground at an angle of 42° above the horizontal with an initial speed of 23 m/s.
   (a) How high will the ball rise?
   (b) How long will it be in the air?
   (c) What will be its range?

6. A baseball is projected horizontally from the top of a building with an initial speed of 15m/s. The ball strikes the ground 25 m from the base of the building.
   (a) How long will it be in the air?
   (b) How tall is the building?

7. Rain is falling vertically down on a car moving at 11 m/s. Tracks made by the raindrops on the side window of the car are inclined at 55° with the vertical. Find the speed of the raindrop relative to the ground.

8. A resting eagle on a tree top finds a rabbit on the ground at a distance of 50 m from the base of the tree. The eagle applies a constant horizontal speed and uses gravity to descend. It catches the rabbit in 2.5 s.
   (a) What is the height of the tree top?
   (b) What is the constant horizontal speed of the eagle?

9. A boat sails in a direction 60° north of east with a constant acceleration of 1.5 m/s^2, starting from rest. What are its northerly and easterly components of the velocity after 15 s?

10. A toy slides down an inclined plane which makes an angle of 60° with the horizontal. It starts from rest and achieves a final velocity of 8 m/s in 5 seconds at the bottom of the plane.
    (a) What is the acceleration down the plane?
    (b) What is the distance along the plane it travels before reaching the bottom of the plane?

11. A ball is thrown horizontally with an initial velocity of 8 m/s, from a height of 50 m above the ground. How long will it take to hit the ground?

12. A stone is thrown horizontally with an initial speed of 3 m/s from a rooftop at a height of 30 m. How far from the base of the building will the stone strike the ground?

13. A toy is thrown horizontally with an initial speed of 5 m/s from the top of a building. It strikes the ground 5 s later. How high is the building?

14. An aircraft is heading at 40° north of east at a speed of 95 m/s relative to the air outside. The wind velocity is 25 m/s due east. Find the magnitude and direction of the velocity of the aircraft with respect to the ground.

15. A rocket is fired with an initial velocity of 200 m/s at an angle of 60° from the ground. How high will the rocket rise?

16. A train moves on a straight track at a speed of 25 m/s. A boy inside the train throws a ball vertically upward from the train floor with a speed of 5 m/s.

(a) What is the magnitude and direction of the velocity of the ball relative to the ground?

(b) What is the range of the ball relative to the train and relative to the ground?

17. After being hit, a golf ball starts at an angle of 35° from the ground with an initial velocity of 70 mph. What will be its range in meters?

18. A projectile is fired at an angle of 60° from the ground. Its range is found to be 500 m. Find its initial velocity.

19. A bullet is fired from a height of 1 m above the ground with a velocity of 85 m/s at an angle of 30° above the horizontal. What will the time of flight of the bullet be before striking the ground?

20. A boy throws a ball with an initial velocity of 20 m/s at an angle of 60° from the top of a building 60 m high. What is the horizontal distance traveled by the ball from the base of the building?

21. An athlete in a high jump competition jumps at an angle of 45° and just crosses over a horizontal bar 2.5 m above the ground. What is the initial speed of the athlete?

22. A rescue plane drops a bag of food and blankets to the victims of an earthquake on the ground. The plane is traveling at a horizontal speed of 25 m/s at a height of 200 m from the ground. What is the horizontal distance the bag travels before striking the ground?

23. A punter kicks a football at an angle of 40°. The ball is airborne for 4 s before hitting the ground. What is the initial speed of the football?

24. A baseball is hit (from close to the mound) with an initial velocity of 33 m/s at an angle of 45° above the horizontal. Will the ball clear a 4 m fence at a distance of 100 m from the mound?

25. A daredevil is thrown from the nozzle (at 3 m from the ground) of a cannon with an initial speed of 20 m/s. His partner holds the net at 2 m from the ground to collect him. The cannon is set at an angle of 45°. How far a horizontal distance should his partner be?

26. A block slides down an inclined plane that makes an angle of 30° with the horizontal with a constant acceleration of 3 m/s². The block starts from rest and travels 5 m along the plane to the bottom. It then continues to move 4 m along the horizontal plane before coming to a stop.

(a) What are the x and y components of the velocity at the bottom of the inclined plane?

(b) What is the deceleration of the block on the horizontal plane?

(c) How long did it take to complete the entire journey?

Check Yourself

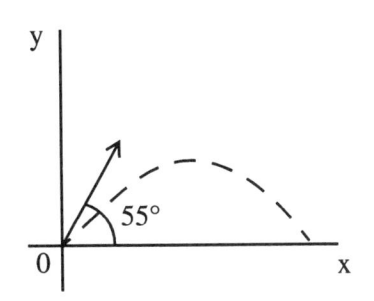

1.

v_{ox} = constant = $v_o \cos\theta_0$ = $22\cos 55°$ = 12.6 m/s

v_{0y} = $v_0 \sin\theta_0$ = $22\sin 55°$ = 18.0 m/s

$v_y = v_{0y} + gt$, $v_y = 18 + (-9.8)2 = -1.6$ m/s

$v = \sqrt{v_x^2 + v_y^2} = [12.6^2 + (-1.6)^2]^{\frac{1}{2}} = 12.7$ m/s

$y = v_{0y}t + \frac{1}{2}gt^2 = 18(2) + \frac{1}{2}(-9.8)2^2$

$y = 16.4$ m

(Projectile motion)

2.

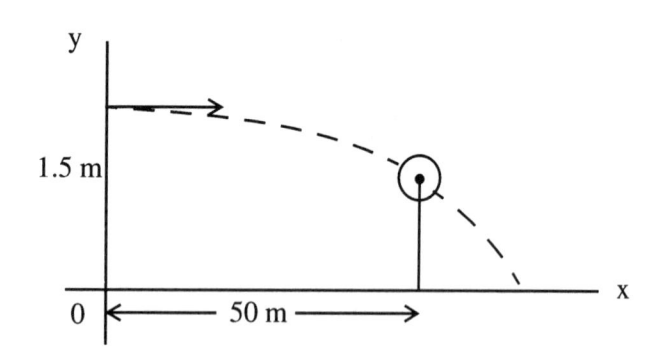

$v_x = v_{0x} = 500$ m/s

$v_{0y} = 0$

$x = v_{0x}t$, $t = \dfrac{x}{v_{0x}} = \dfrac{50}{500} = 1\times10^{-1}$ s

$y = v_{oy}t + \frac{1}{2}gt^2 = 0 + \frac{1}{2}(-9.8)(1\times10^{-1})^2 = -4.9\times10^{-2}$ m

Height = $1.5 - 4.9\times10^{-2} = 1.45$ m

(Projectile motion)

3.

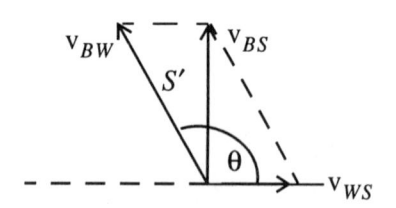

Speed of water relative to shore = v_{WS} = 5 mi/hr = 2.2 m/s

Speed of boat relative to water = v_{BW}

Speed of boat relative to shore = v_{BS} = 15 mi/hr = 6.7 m/s

$$\mathbf{v}_{BS} = \mathbf{v}_{BW} + \mathbf{v}_{WS}, \quad \mathbf{v}_{BW} = \mathbf{v}_{BS} - \mathbf{v}_{WS}$$

$$(v_{BW})_x = (v_{BS})_x - (v_{WS})_x = 0 - 2.2 = -2.2 \text{ m/s}$$

$$(v_{BW})_y = (v_{BS})_y - (v_{WS})_y = 6.7 - 0 = 6.7 \text{ m/s}$$

$$\theta = \tan^{-1}\left[\frac{(v_{BW})_y}{(v_{BW})_x}\right] = \tan^{-1}\left(\frac{6.7}{-2.2}\right) = -72°$$

So the angle is 108°

$$v_{BW} = \sqrt{(-2.2)^2 + (6.7)^2} = \pm 7.0 \text{ m/s}$$

$$v_{BW} = 15.7 \text{ mph}$$

Velocity relative to shore is 15.7 mph at 108°.

(Relative velocity)

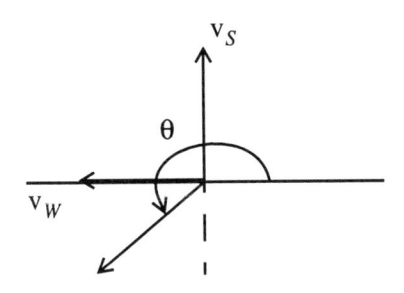

4.

v_s = velocity of ship = 6 m/s

v_w = velocity of wind = 2.5 m/s

v = Resultant Velocity of the two.

$$v_x = v\cos\theta = v_w$$

$$v_y = v\sin\theta = v_s$$

$$\frac{v_y}{v_x} = \frac{v\sin\theta}{v\cos\theta} = \frac{v_s}{v_w}$$

$$\tan\theta = \frac{v_s}{v_w}, \quad \theta = \tan^{-1}\left(\frac{v_s}{v_w}\right)$$

$$\theta = \tan^{-1}\left(\frac{6}{2.5}\right) = 67.4°$$

Pennant will fly at 247.4° or 67.4° south of west.

(Motion in a plane)

5. (a)

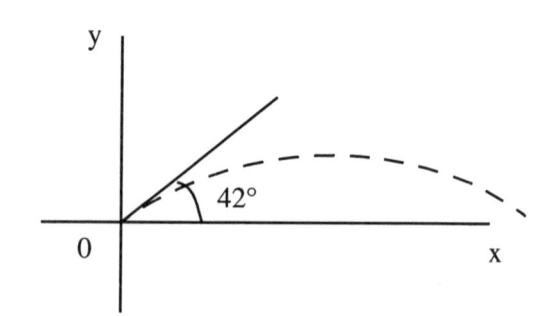

$v_0 = 23$ m/s

$\theta_0 = 42°$

$v_x = v_{0x} = v_0 \cos\theta_0 = 23\cos 42° = 17.1$ m/s

$v_{oy} = v_0 \sin\theta_0 = 23\sin 42° = 15.4$ m/s

$v_y^2 = v_{0y}^2 + 2gy$

$0 = 15.4^2 + 2(-9.8)y$

$y = 12.1$ m

(b) $v_y = v_{0y} + gt$

$0 = 15.4 + (-9.8)t$

$t = \dfrac{15.4}{9.8} = 1.57$

$2t = 3.1 s$

(c) Range $= x = v_{ox}t = (17.1)(3.1) = 53$ m

(Projectile motion)

6. (a)

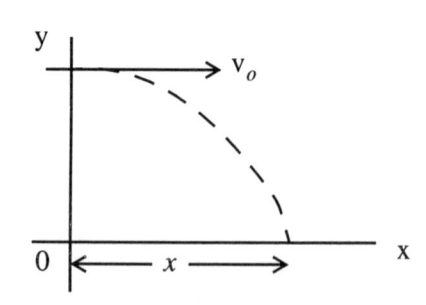

$v_0 = 15$ m/s, $\theta_0 = 0°$ and $x = 25$ m

$x = v_{0x}t$, $\dfrac{x}{v_{0x}} = \dfrac{25}{15} = 1.67 s$

(b) $y = v_{0y}t + \frac{1}{2}gt^2$

$y = 0 + \frac{1}{2}(-9.8)(1.67)^2$

$y = -13.7$ m

So, the building is 13.7 m high.

(Projectile motion)

7.

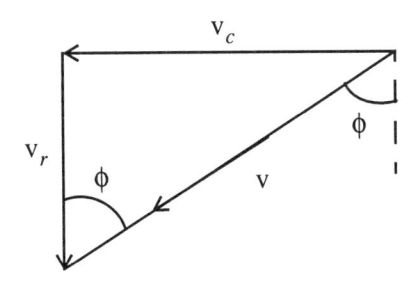

v_c = velocity of car relative to ground = 11 m/s

v_r = velocity of raindrops relative to ground

v = velocity of raindrops relative to car

$\tan\phi = \dfrac{v_c}{v_r}$

$v_r = \dfrac{v_c}{\tan\phi} = \dfrac{11}{\tan 55°} = 7.7$ m/s

(Relative velocity)

8. (a) v_x = constant horizontal speed of the eagle

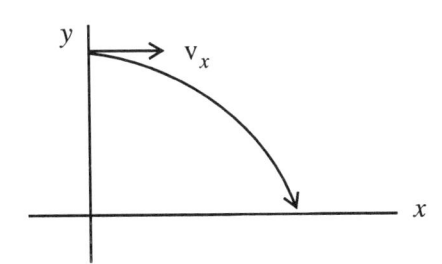

$v_{oy} = 0$, $a_y = g = -9.8$ m/s^2

$t = 2.5 s$

$$y = v_{oy}t + \frac{1}{2}gt^2 = 0 + \frac{1}{2}(-9.8)2.5^2$$

$$y = -30.6 \text{ m}$$

Height of the tree is 30.6 m.

(b) $x = v_{0x}t = v_x t$

$$v_x = \frac{x}{t} = \frac{50}{2.5} = 20 \text{ m/s}$$

Horizontal speed of the eagle is 20 m/s.

(Projectile motion)

9.

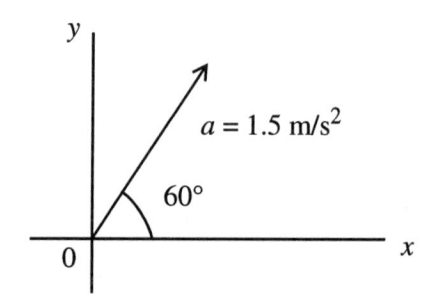

$a_x = a\cos 60° = 1.5\cos 60° = 0.75 \text{ m/s}^2$

$a_y = a\sin 60° = 1.5\sin 60° = 1.3 \text{ m/s}^2$

$t = 15s$

$v_x = v_{0x} + a_x t$

$v_x = 0 + 0.75 \times 15 = 11.2 \text{ m/s}$

$v_y = v_{oy} + a_y t = 0 + 1.3 \times 15 = 19.5 \text{ m/s}$

11.2 m/s is easterly component of the velocity.

19.5 m/s is northerly component of the velocity.

(Motion in a plane)

10. (a)

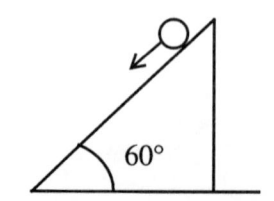

$$v = v_0 + at$$

$$8 = 0 + a(5)$$

$$a = 1.6 \text{ m/s}^2$$

(b) $x = v_{0x}t + \frac{1}{2}at^2$

$$x = 0 + \frac{1}{2}(1.6)5^2$$

$$x = 20 \text{ m}$$

(Motion in a plane)

11.

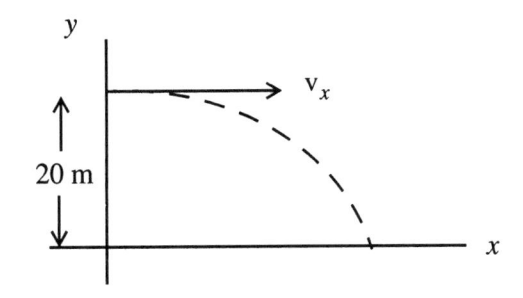

$$v_{0x} = v_x = 8 \text{ m/s},$$

$$v_{0y} = 0$$

$$v_y^2 = v_{0y}^2 + 2gy = 0 + 2(-9.8)(-50)$$

$$v_y^2 = 980, \ v_y = \pm 31.3$$

$$v_y = 31.3 \text{ m/s downward}$$

$$v_y = v_{0y} + gt$$

$$-31.3 = 0 + (-9.8)t$$

$$t = \frac{31.3}{9.8} = 3.2 s$$

It will take 3.2 s.

(Projectile motion)

12. As in problem number 11,

$$v_y^2 = v_{oy}^2 + 2gy = 2(-9.8)(-30) = 588$$

$$v_y = \pm 24.2$$

$$v_y = v_{oy} + gt$$

$$-24.2 = 0 + (-9.8)t$$

$$t = 2.5 s$$

$$x = v_{ox}t = 3 \times 2.5 = 7.4 \text{ m}$$

The stone will strike the ground at 7.4 m from the base of the building.

(Projectile motion)

13. $$y = v_{oy}t + \frac{1}{2}gt^2$$

$$= 0 + \frac{1}{2}(-9.8)5^2$$

$$= -122.5 \text{ m}$$

The building is 122.5 m high (note that the horizontal velocity is irrelevant to the solution).

(Projectile motion)

14.

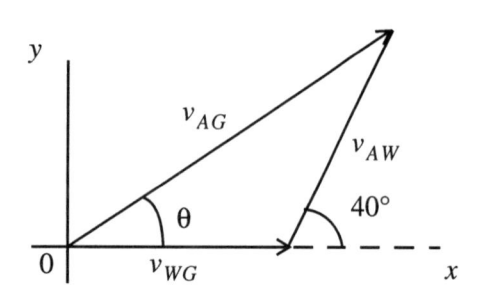

$\mathbf{v}_{AW}$ = Velocity of aircraft relative to wind

$\mathbf{v}_{WG}$ = Velocity of wind relative to ground

$\mathbf{v}_{AG}$ = Velocity of aircraft relative to ground

$$\mathbf{v}_{AG} = \mathbf{v}_{AW} + \mathbf{v}_{WG}$$

Equating the x-components we have,

$$(v_{AG})_x = (v_{AW})_x + (v_{WG})_x$$

$$= (v_{AW})\cos\theta_1 + (v_{WG})\cos\theta_2$$

$$= 95 \cos 40° + 25 \cos 0°$$

$$= 72.8 + 25 = 97.8 \text{ m/s}$$

Motion in Two Dimensions / 49

And, $(v_{AG})_y = (v_{AW})_y + (v_{WG})_y$

$= 95 \sin 40° + 25 \sin 0°$

$= 61.1 + 0$

$= 61.1$ m/s

$v_{AG} = \sqrt{(v_{AG})_x^2 + (v_{AG})_y^2} = [97.8^2 + 61.1^2]^{1/2} = \pm 115.3$

$\theta = \tan^{-1}\left(\dfrac{61.1}{97.8}\right) = 32°$

115.3 m/s at 32° north of east

(Relative velocity)

15.

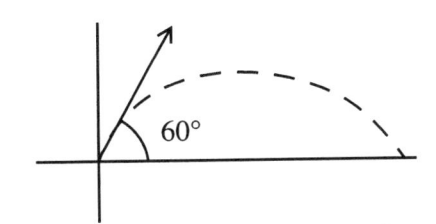

$v_o = 200$ m/s

$\theta_o = 60°$

$v_{oy} = v_o \sin \theta_o = 200 \sin 60° = 173.2$

$v_y^2 = v_{oy}^2 + 2gy$

$0 = (173.2)^2 + 2(-9.8)y$

$y = 1.53 \times 10^3$ m

(Projectile motion)

16. (a)

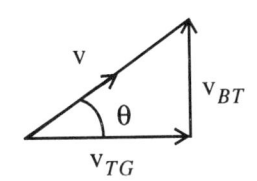

v_{BT} = velocity of the ball relative to train

v_{TG} = velocity of train relative to ground

v = velocity of ball relative to ground

$$v^2 = v_{BT}^2 + v_{TG}^2$$

$$v^2 = 5^2 + 25^2$$

$$v = \sqrt{25 + 625} = \pm 25.5$$

$$\theta = \tan^{-1}\left(\frac{v_{BT}}{v_{TG}}\right) = \tan^{-1}\left(\frac{5}{25}\right) = 11.3$$

The velocity of the ball relative to the ground is 25.5 m/s at 11.3°.

(b) Range is zero relative to train.

$$v_y = v_{oy} + gt$$

$$0 = 5 - 9.8t$$

$$t = 0.51 \text{ s}$$

Time of flight $= 2t = 1.02$ s

$$x = v_{ox}t = (25)1.02 = 25.5 \text{ m}$$

Range is 25.5 m relative to the ground.

(Relative velocity)

17. 1 mph $= 0.447$ m/s

70 mph $= 31.3$ m/s

$$v_o = 31.3 \text{ m/s}$$

$$\theta_o = 35°$$

$$v_y = v_{oy} + gt$$

$$0 = (v_o \sin\theta_o) - 9.8t$$

$$t = \frac{v_o \sin\theta_o}{9.8} = \frac{31.3 \sin 35°}{9.8} = 1.83 \text{ s}$$

Range,

$$x = v_{ox}t = (v_o \cos\theta_o)(2 \times 1.83) = (31.3 \cos 35°)(2 \times 1.83) = 93.8 \text{ m}$$

(Projectile motion)

18. $$v_y = v_{oy} + gt$$

$$0 = v_o \sin\theta_o + gt$$

$$t = -\frac{v_o \sin\theta_o}{g}$$

$$x = v_{ox}(2t) = 2(v_o\cos\theta_o)\frac{-v_o\sin\theta_o}{g}$$

$$x = -\frac{2v_o^2\sin\theta_o\cos\theta_o}{g}$$

$$500 = -\frac{2v_o^2\sin 60°\cos 60°}{(-9.8)}$$

$$v_o^2 = \frac{500 \times 9.8}{2\sin 60°\cos 60°} = 5.66\times 10^3$$

$$v_o = \pm 75.2$$

Initial velocity of the projectile is 75.2 m/s at 60°.

(Projectile motion)

19.

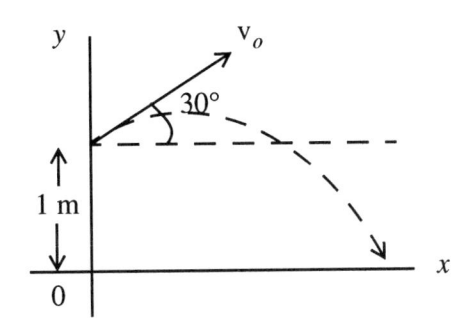

$$v_{oy} = v_o\sin\theta_o = 85\sin 30° = 42.5 \text{ m/s}$$

Here the height fallen through is 1 m below the initial point.

$$y = v_{oy}t + \frac{1}{2}gt^2$$

$$-1 = 42.5t + \frac{1}{2}(-9.8)t^2$$

$$4.9t^2 - 42.5t - 1 = 0 \quad \text{Solution of quadratic equation } \left[x = \frac{-b\pm\sqrt{b^2-4ac}}{2a}\right]$$

$$t = \frac{42.5}{2\times 4.9} \pm \frac{[42.5^2 - 4(4.9)(-1)]^{1/2}}{2\times 4.9} = 4.34 \pm \frac{42.7}{9.8}$$

$t = 4.34 \pm 4.36 = 8.7$ s (the solution $t = -0.02$ s would be unrealistic)

Time of flight is 8.7 s.

(Projectile motion)

52 / Physics I

20.

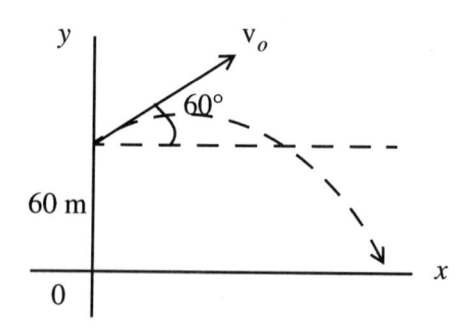

$v_o = 20$ m/s, $\theta_o = 60°$

$v_{ox} = v_o \cos\theta_o = 20 \cos 60° = 10$ m/s

$v_{oy} = v_o \sin\theta_o = 20 \sin 60° = 17.3$ m/s

$v_y^2 = v_{oy}^2 + 2gy$

$v_y^2 = 17.3^2 + 2(-9.8)(-60) = 2.99 \times 10^2 + 1176$

$v_y = \pm 38.4$

Final velocity is vertically down and hence negative.

$v_y = -38.4$ m/s

$v_y = v_{oy} + gt$

$-38.4 = 17.3 + (-9.8)t$

$t = \dfrac{17.3 + 38.4}{9.8} = 5.68$ s

$x = v_{ox}t = (10)5.68 = 56.8$ m

(Projectile motion)

21.

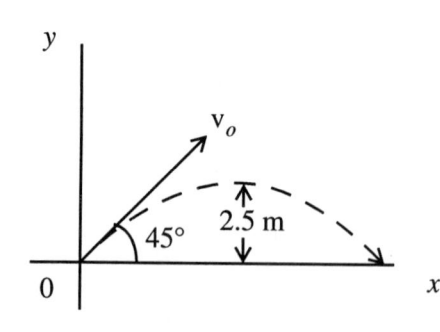

$v_y^2 = v_{oy}^2 + 2gy$

$0 = v_{oy}^2 + 2(-9.8)2.5$

$$v_{oy}^2 = 49$$

$$v_{oy} = \pm 7, \; v_{oy} = 7 \text{ m/s}$$

$$v_{oy} = v_o \sin\theta_o$$

$$v_o = \frac{v_{oy}}{\sin\theta_o} = \frac{7}{\sin 45°} = 9.9 \text{ m/s}$$

(Projectile motion)

22.

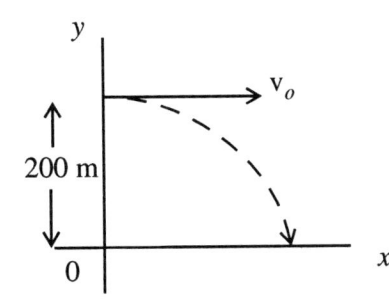

$$v_{ox} = v_o = 25 \text{ m/s}, \; v_{oy} = 0$$

$$y = v_{oy}t + \frac{1}{2}gt^2$$

$$-200 = 0 + \frac{1}{2}(-9.8)t^2$$

$$4.9t^2 = 200$$

$$t = \pm 6.4$$

$$x = v_{ox}t = 25 \times 6.4 = 158 \text{ m}$$

(Projectile motion)

23.

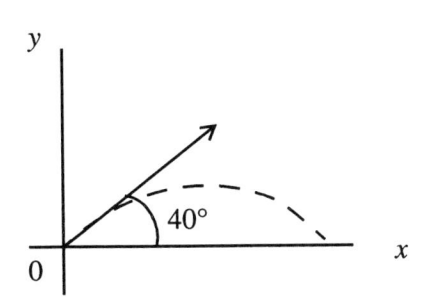

$$y = (v_o \sin\theta_o)t + \frac{1}{2}gt^2$$

$$0 = (v_o \sin 40°)4 + \frac{1}{2}(-9.8)4^2$$

$$0 = 2.57 v_o - 78.4$$

$$v_o = 30.5 \text{ m/s}$$

(Projectile motion)

24.

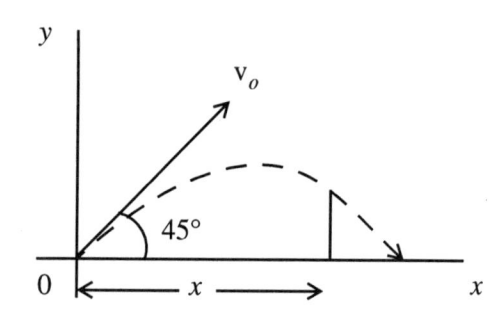

$$v_{ox} = v_o \cos 45° = 33 \cos 45° = 23.3 \text{ m/s}$$

$$v_{oy} = v_o \sin 45° = 33 \sin 45° = 23.3 \text{ m/s}$$

$$x = v_{ox} t$$

$$100 = 23.3 t$$

$$t = 4.29 \text{ s}$$

$$y = v_{oy} t + \frac{1}{2} g t^2 = (23.3)4.29 + \frac{1}{2}(-9.8)4.29^2$$

$$y = 99.96 - 90.18 = 9.78 \text{ m}$$

It will clear the 4 m fence.

(Projectile motion)

25.

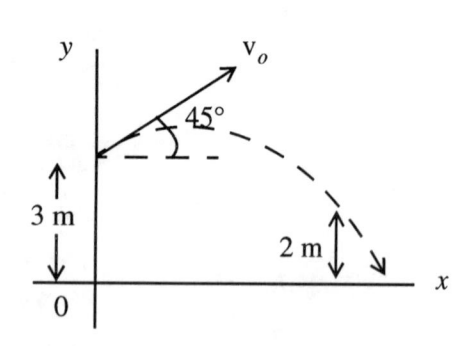

$$v_{ox} = v_o \cos 45° = 20(\cos 45°) = 14.1 \text{ m/s}$$

$$v_{oy} = v_o \sin 45° = 20(\sin 45°) = 14.1 \text{ m/s}$$

$y = y_2 - y_1 = 2 - 3 = -1$ m

$v_y^2 = v_{oy}^2 + 2gy$

$v_y^2 = 14.1^2 - 2(9.8)(-1) = 218.4$

$v_y = \pm 14.8$

so, $v_y = -14.8$ m/s (– sign being downward)

$v_y = v_{oy} + gt$

$-14.8 = 14.1 + (-9.8)t$

$9.8t = 14.1 + 14.8 = 28.9$

$t = 2.95$ s

$x = v_{ox}t = 14.1 \times 2.95 = 41.6$ m

(Projectile motion)

26. (a)

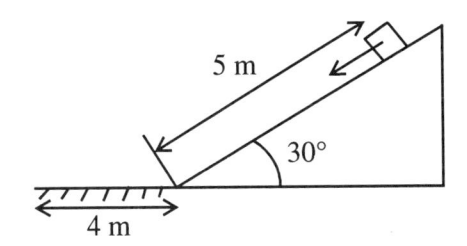

$v^2 = v_o^2 + 2ax$

$v^2 = 0 + 2(3)5 = 30$

$v = \pm 5.5$

$v_x = v\cos\theta = 5.5 \cos 30° = 4.76$ m/s

$v_y = v\sin\theta = 5.5 \sin 30° = 2.75$ m/s

(b) $v_x^2 = v_{ox}^2 + 2ax$

$a = \dfrac{v_x^2 - v_{ox}^2}{2x} = \dfrac{0 - 4.76^2}{2 \times 4} = -2.8$ m/s²

(c) $v = v_o + at_1$

$t_1 = \dfrac{v - v_o}{a} = \dfrac{5.5 - 0}{3} = 1.8$ s

$$v = v_o + at_2$$

$$0 = 4.76 - 2.8t_2$$

$$t_2 = \frac{4.76}{2.8} = 1.7 \text{ s}$$

Time = $t_1 + t_2$ = 3.5 s

(Motion in a plane)

Grade Yourself

Circle the question numbers that you had incorrect. Then indicate the number of questions you missed. If you answered more than three questions incorrectly, you need to focus on that topic. (If a topic has less than three questions and you had at least one wrong, we suggest you study that topic also. Read your textbook, a review book, or ask your teacher for help.)

Subject: Motion in Two Dimensions

Topic	Question Numbers	Number Incorrect
Motion in a plane	4, 9, 10, 26	
Relative velocity	3, 7, 14, 16	
Projectile motion	1, 2, 5, 6, 8, 11, 12, 13, 15, 17, 18, 19, 20, 21, 22, 23, 24, 25	

Force and Motion

5

Brief Yourself

The state of an object whether in motion or at rest can only be changed by the use of force. This brings out Newton's first law, referred to as the Law of Inertia.

The uniform acceleration you studied in one and two dimensions in Chapters 2 and 4 must ultimately be caused by some kind of force. The basic relation of force is given in Newton's second law:

$$\mathbf{F} = m\mathbf{a} \qquad (1)$$

where $\mathbf{F}$, m, and $\mathbf{a}$ stand for force, mass, and acceleration, respectively. The force is a vector, and therefore vector algebra applies to all relations involving force. For a single force, its components are given by:

$F_x = ma_x$

$F_y = ma_y$

If two or more forces act on a body, the resultant force is the sum of all forces acting on the body. For example, the resultant force $\mathbf{F}$ of three forces is:

$$\mathbf{F} = \mathbf{F}_1 + \mathbf{F}_2 + \mathbf{F}_3 \qquad (2)$$

where $\mathbf{F}_1$, $\mathbf{F}_2$, and $\mathbf{F}_3$ are the three individual forces. The x and y components of the forces in equation (2) add in the following way:

$F_x = ma_x = F_{1x} + F_{2x} + F_{3x}$

$F_y = ma_y = F_{1y} + F_{2y} + F_{3y}$

The magnitude of the resultant force is:

$F = [F_x^2 + F_y^2]^{1/2}$

while the direction of the resultant force is,

$\theta = \tan^{-1}[F_y/F_x]$

When the resultant force is zero, one finds:

$F_{1x} + F_{2x} + F_{3x} = 0$

$F_{1y} + F_{2y} + F_{3y} = 0$

You need to be familiar with some of the common forces around you. These are forces such as external or applied force (e.g., pushing or pulling), force of gravity, and the force of friction. In the case of gravity, the force is given by:

F = mg (3)

where **g** is the acceleration due to gravity.

The relation for the force of friction is written in a different form.

f = μN (4)

where f, μ and N stand for the force of friction, the coefficient of friction, and the normal force. There are two kinds of friction, namely static and kinetic. The value of the coefficient of friction m changes with the kind of force of friction.

There are some oft quoted examples of motion under force. These are examples as in the Atwood Machine (two blocks over a pulley) and the inclined plane problem.

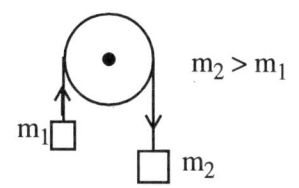

Figure: Atwood Machine

When two blocks (m_1 and m_2) tied to the two ends of a massless string that runs over a frictionless pulley, are in motion, the acceleration of any one block is:

$a = [(m_1 - m_2)/(m_1 + m_2)]g$ (5)

and the tension T in the string is:

$T = [2m_1 m_2/(m_1 + m_2)]g$ (6)

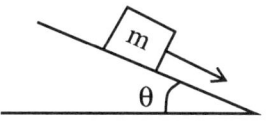

Figure: Inclined Plane

In the inclined plane problem, the acceleration caused by gravity down the inclined plane is:

a = g sin θ

and the normal force on the block is:

N = mg cos θ

where m is the mass of the block and θ is the angle of the inclined plane made with the horizontal.

Test Yourself

1. Find the force required to produce an acceleration of 1.5 m/s² on a body of mass 25 kg.

2. A sled of mass 100 kg decelerates at 0.4 m/s² while coasting over the ice. What is the retarding force of friction due to ice?

3. A block of mass 15 kg placed on a smooth horizontal plane is pushed with a force of 22 N parallel to the plane. What is the acceleration of the block?

4. An automobile of mass 1,500 kg moving on level ground at a speed of 33 m/s comes to a halt in a distance of 50 m. What average force of the brakes did the driver apply?

5. An elevator weighs 40,000 Newtons and the tension in the cable supporting the elevator is 35,000 Newtons. What is the acceleration of the elevator?

6. A 0.15 kg bullet starting from rest achieves a final velocity of 550 m/s while traveling 0.33 m in the barrel of a gun. Calculate the average force exerted on the bullet.

7. A bowling ball is released with a final velocity of 7 m/s after it accelerates uniformly for 0.5 seconds starting from rest. The mass of the ball is 8 kg. How much force is exerted by the bowler?

8. A 70 kg skydiver freely descends downward while experiencing an upward air resistance of 260 N. How long will she take to descend 100 m if her initial velocity is 10 m/s downward?

9. The mass of a spider is 10 grams. A vertical strand of silk supports part of its weight with 0.075 N of force. What is the net force acting on the spider?

10. A 135 kg person caught in a fire in a hotel room climbs down the window of his room with a rope that can sustain a tension of no more than 1000 N. What is the minimum acceleration the man must maintain to land safely on the ground without breaking the rope?

11. In a car accident, a wreckless driver may die due to a sudden deceleration of about 30 times greater than gravity. What would be the force of such deceleration on a driver of mass 75 kg?

12. In a circus show, clown A (110 kg) and clown B (125 kg) are tied to the two ends of a rope and vertically suspended over a frictionless pulley as shown below. Find the acceleration of each clown and tension in the string.

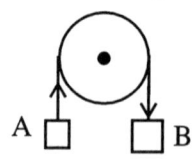

13. A 15-ton engine pulls a 100-ton train with an acceleration of 5 m/s². What acceleration would the same engine produce if pulling a 75-ton train?

14. A helicopter in a rescue operation accelerates upward at 5 m/s², lifting a victim with a mass of 95 kg who holds a rope tied to the aircraft. What tension must the rope provide if the victim can't help dangling at the end of the rope?

15. In some animals, the heart pumps out 25 cc of blood (Density = 1.1 g/cc) in 0.2 s while the speed of the blood flow increases from 27 cm/s to 35 cm/s. What is the force exerted by the muscle of the heart?

16. A passenger with a mass of 120 kg rides an elevator that accelerates upward with an acceleration of 2 m/s². How heavy does the passenger feel?

17. A lady with a mass of 75 kg rides an elevator that is accelerating downward at 1.5 m/s². How light does she feel?

18. A block with a mass of 5 kg is placed on a flat horizontal table. It moves parallel to the table top with an acceleration of 2.5 m/s² when pushed with a horizontal force. Find the horizontal force applied on the block if the

    (a) force of friction is not present
    (b) coefficient of friction is equal to 0.2 between the block and table.

19. A skier with a mass of 130 kg slides downhill (25° below the horizontal) accelerating at 5 m/s².

What is the force applied by the skier down the plane in the absence of friction?

20. Three co-planar forces are acting on a body with a mass of 85 kg. The first force is 15 N at 0°, the second 25 N at 125° and the third 65 N at 210°. Find the resultant force in magnitude and direction.

21. An astronaut weighing 1,150 N on earth experiences an acceleration of 1.96 m/s² due to the Moon's gravity on the lunar surface. What would be the astronaut's mass and weight on the Moon?

22. Find the force exerted by the floor of the elevator on a 75 kg passenger standing on it, if the elevator is,

    (a) at rest
    (b) going up at constant velocity of 4 m/s
    (c) moving up at an acceleration of 1.3 m/s²
    (d) moving up but decelerating at 2.0 m/s²
    (e) going down with a deceleration of 1.5 m/s².

23. A 145 kg sled is pulled by a rope with a force of 500 N on icy level ground. The force is directed at an angle of 40° with the horizontal. The coefficient of friction is 0.1 between sled and ice. Find the acceleration of the sled.

24. A 25 kg block moves at constant speed up an inclined plane which makes an angle of 25° with the horizontal. The coefficient of sliding friction is 0.28 between the block and the plane. Find the applied force on the block parallel to the inclined plane.

25. A block slides down a rough plane inclined at 35°. Find the acceleration of the block if the coefficient of sliding friction is 0.15.

26. What is the maximum acceleration of a car moving without slipping if the coefficient of friction is 0.5 between the tires of the car and the ground?

27. A truck carries a heavy crate containing 2,500 kg of machinery on a flatbed at its rear. How fast may the driver of the truck accelerate safely without disturbing the crate? The coefficient of friction is 0.35 between the crate and the flatbed.

28. A traffic light with a mass of 65 kg is vertically suspended by three cables as shown below. Tension T_1 makes an angle of 30° and tension T_2 makes an angle of 40° as shown. Find the two tensions T_1 and T_2.

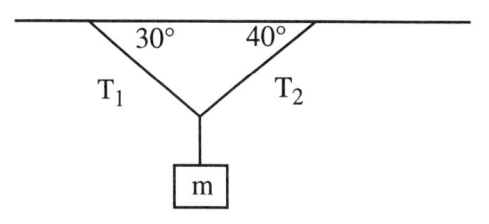

29. A block with a mass of 3 kg, placed on a horizontal table top, is pulled by a horizontal string running over a frictionless pulley set at the edge of the table (as shown below). The free end of the string is tied to a block of mass 8 kg suspended vertically and pulling the other block. Find the acceleration of each block if,

    (a) the table top is frictionless
    (b) the coefficient of friction is 0.25 between the block and table top.

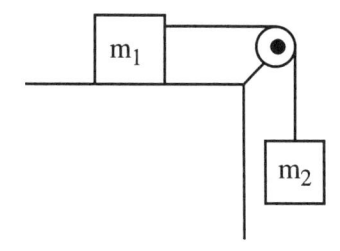

30. Two blocks, each with a mass of 12 kg, are tied to the two ends of a cable which runs over a frictionless pulley set at the top of an inclined plane as shown below. The inclined plane is frictionless and makes an angle of 33° with the horizontal. Find the acceleration of the blocks and the tension in the cable.

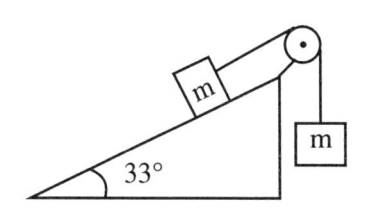

Check Yourself

1. Mass, $m = 25$ kg, Acceleration $a = 1.5$ m/s²

   Force $F = ma$

   $F = 25 \times 1.5 = 37.5$ N

   (Force in general)

2. Mass $m = 100$ kg

   Deceleration $a = -0.4$ m/s²

   Force $= ma = 100(-0.4) = -40.0$ N

   40 N opposing the motion.

   (Force in general)

3. Mass, $m = 15$ kg

   Force, $F = 22$ N

   $F = ma, \ a = \dfrac{F}{m} = \dfrac{22}{15} = 1.47$ m/s²

   (Force in general)

4. $$v^2 = v_0^2 + 2ax$$

   $$0 = 33^2 + 2(a)50$$

   $$a = -\dfrac{33^2}{2 \times 50} = -10.9 \text{ m/s}^2$$

   Average force $F = ma = 1500 \times (-10.9)$

   $$F = -1.63 \times 10^4 \text{ N}$$

   16.3 kilonewtons of force

   (Force in general)

5. Force of gravity, $W = mg = 40,000$ N

   Tension upward, $T = 35,000$ N

   Net Force, $F = T - W$

   $= 35,000 - 40,000$

   $F = -5000$ N downward

Mass of elevator, $M = \dfrac{W}{g} = \dfrac{40,000}{9.8} = 4,081.6$ kg

Acceleration, $a = \dfrac{F}{m} = \dfrac{-5,000}{4081.6} = -1.2$ m/s^2.

Acceleration is downward at 1.2 m/s^2.

(Application of Newton's Laws)

6. $v^2 = v_0^2 + 2ax$

   $550^2 = 0 + 2(a)(0.33)$

   $a = \dfrac{550^2}{2 \times 0.33} = 4.58 \times 10^5$ m/s^2

   $F = ma = 0.15 \times 4.58 \times 10^5 = 6.87 \times 10^4$ N

(Force in general)

7. $v = v_0 + at$

   $7 = 0 + a(0.5)$

   $a = \dfrac{7}{0.5} = 14$ m/s^2

   $F = ma = 8 \times 14 = 112$ N

(Force in general)

8. Force of gravity, $W = mg = 70 \times 9.8$

   $W = 686$ N

   Air resistance $= R = 260$ N

   Net force, $F = R - W = 260 - 686$

   $F = -426$ N

   $a = \dfrac{F}{m} = \dfrac{-426}{70} = -6.08$ m/s^2

   $v^2 = v_0^2 + 2ax$

   $v^2 = (-10)^2 + 2(-6.08)(-100) = 1316$

   $v = \pm 36.3$

   $v = -36.3$ m/s

   $v = v_0 + at$

$$-36.3 = -10 + (-6.08)t$$

$$t = \frac{-26.3}{-6.08} = 4.3 \text{ s}$$

(Application of Newton's Laws)

9. Mass = 10 g = 0.01 kg

   $W = mg = (0.01)9.8 = 0.098$ N

   supporting force of silk, $S = 0.075$ N

   Net force, $F = S - W = 0.075 - 0.098$

   $$F = -0.023 \text{ N}$$

   Net force is 0.023 N downward.

(Force in general)

10. Force of gravity, $W = mg = 135 \times 9.8 = 1323$ N

    Tension, $T = 1,000$ N

    Net force, $F = T - W = 1,000 - 1,323$

    $$F = -323 \text{ N}$$

    Acceleration, $a = \dfrac{F}{m} = \dfrac{-323}{135} = -2.4$ m/s^2

    The person must maintain a 2.4 m/s^2 acceleration downward to reach the ground safely.

(Application of Newton's Laws)

11. Deceleration = $30 \times g = 30 \times 9.8 = 294$ m/s^2

    $F = ma = 75 \times (-294) = -2.2 \times 10^4$ N

    Force on the victim is 22 kilonewtons.

(Force in general)

12. Free body force diagram of clown A is

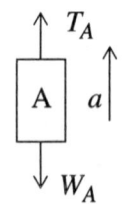

    Net force on clown A is upward

    $$F_A = T_A - W_A$$

$$m_A a = T_A - m_A g \qquad (1)$$

Acceleration a is upward

Free body force diagram of clown B is

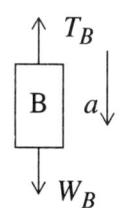

Net force on clown B is downward
(note accleration has a minus sign),

$$F_B = T_B - W_B$$

Note acceleration a is downward.

$$m_B(-a) = T_B - m_B g$$

$$-m_B a = T_B - m_B g \qquad (2)$$

Tensions T_A and T_B are the same.

Let $T = T_A = T_B$

Rewriting equations (1) and (2) we get

$$m_A a = T - m_A g \qquad (3)$$

$$-m_B a = T - m_B g \qquad (4)$$

Subtracting equation (4) from (3), $(m_A + m_B)a = -m_A g + m_B g$

$$a = \frac{m_B g - m_A g}{m_A + m_B}$$

$$a = \frac{(m_B - m_A)g}{m_A + m_B} = \frac{125 - 110}{125 + 110} \times 9.8$$

$$= 0.62 \text{ m/s}^2$$

clown A accelerates upward at 0.62 m/s^2

and clown B accelerates downward at 0.62 m/s^2.

From equation (3), $m_A a = T - m_A g$

$(110)(0.62) = T - (110)(9.8)$

Tension, $T = 110 \times 0.62 + 110 \times 9.8 = 1146$ N

(Application of Newton's Laws)

13. $F_1 = m_1 a_1$

    $F_2 = m_2 a_2$

    Here the force of the engine is the same.

    $F_1 = F_2 = F$

    $m_1 a_1 = m_2 a_2$

    $\dfrac{a_2}{a_1} = \dfrac{m_1}{m_2}$

    $a_2 = (a_1)\dfrac{m_1}{m_2} = (5)\left(\dfrac{100}{75}\right) = 6.7$ m/s^2

(Force in general)

14. Free body force diagram is,

    Net force, $F = T - W$

    $ma = T + -mg$

    $T = ma + mg = m(a + g)$

    $T = 95(5 + 9.8)$

    $T = 1406$ N

(Application of Newton's Laws)

15. $v = v_0 + at$

    $35 = 27 + (a)(0.2)$

    $a = \dfrac{35 - 27}{0.2} = 40 \,\dfrac{\text{cm}}{\text{s}^2} = 0.4 \,\dfrac{\text{m}}{\text{s}^2}$

Force, $F = ma$

Here, density $D = \frac{m}{V}$, $m = DV = (1.1)(25) = 27.5$ g $= 0.0275$ kg

Force $= ma$

$F = 0.0275 \times 0.4$

$= 1.1 \times 10^{-2}$ N

Muscle exerts 1.1×10^{-2} N of force.

(Force in general)

16. Here, free body force diagram of the passenger is,

At rest, elevator floor exerts a force equal to force of gravity.

That is, $F_{fl} = W$

When elevator accelerates, floor of the elevator accelerates at 2 m/s² and exerts additional force. So,

$F_{fl} = W + ma = 120 \times 9.8 + 120 \times 2$

$F_{fl} = 1176 + 240 = 1416$ N

Apparent mass, $m_a = \dfrac{F_{fl}}{g} = \dfrac{1416}{9.8} = 144.5$ kg

(Application of Newton's Laws)

17.

F_{fl} = Force upward of elevator floor.

The net force on the Lady is,

$$F = F_{fl} - W$$

$$-ma = F_{fl} - mg \text{ (Negative sign because net acceleration is downward)}$$

$$F_{fl} = mg - ma = m(g - a)$$

$$= 75(9.8 - 1.5) = 75 \times 8.3 = 622.5 \text{ N}$$

Mass = $\dfrac{w}{g}$

Apparent mass = 63.5 kg

Mass difference = 11.5 kg, lighter

(Application of Newton's Laws)

18.

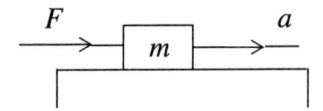

(a) Net force, $F = ma$

$$F = 5 \times 2.5 = 12.5 \text{ N}$$

(b) Net force, $F = F_1 - f$ \hfill (1)

F_1 = Applied force

f = Force of friction

$f = \mu N$, N is Normal force, μ is coefficient of friction

Sum of vertical forces is zero.

That is, $0 = N - W$

$$N = W = mg$$

So, $f = \mu N = \mu mg$

From equation (1), we have

$$F = F_1 - \mu mg$$

$$F_1 = F + \mu mg = ma + \mu mg$$

$$F_1 = 5 \times 2.5 + 0.2 \times 5 \times 9.8$$

$$F_1 = 12.5 + 9.8 = 22.3 \text{ N}$$

(Application of Newton's Laws)

19.

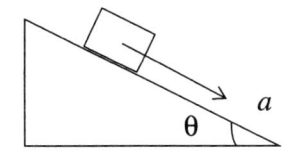

Force of gravity down the plane is,

$W_D = mg\sin\theta$

If applied force of the skier down the plane is F_1, then net force

$F = F_1 + W_D$

$F_1 = F - W_D = ma - mg\sin\theta$

$F_1 = (130 \times 5) - 130 \times 9.8(\sin 25°)$

$\quad = 650 - 538.4$

$F_1 = 111.5$ N

(Application of Newton's Laws)

20.

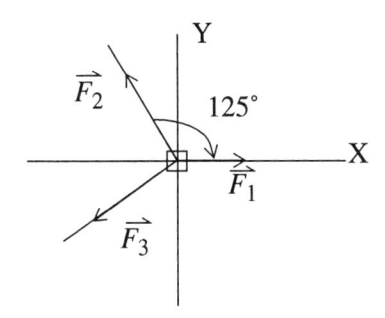

The three forces are

$F_1 = 15$ N at $0°$

$F_2 = 25$ N at $125°$

$F_3 = 65$ N at $210°$

Sum of the forces along the x-axis is,

$R_x = F_{1x} + F_{2x} + F_{3x}$

$R_x = F_1\cos\theta_1 + F_2\cos\theta_2 + F_3\cos\theta_3$

$R_x = 15\cos 0° + 25\cos 125° + 65\cos 210°$

$R_x = 15 - 14.3 - 56.3$

$R_x = -55.6$ N

Similarly, sum along the y-axis is,

$R_y = F_{1y} + F_{2y} + F_{3y}$

$= F_1 \sin\theta_1 + F_2 \sin\theta_2 + F \sin\theta_3$

$= 15\sin 0° + 25\sin 125° + 65\sin 210°$

$= 0 + 20.5 - 32.5$

$R_y = -12$ N

$R = (R_x^2 + R_y^2)^{1/2} = [(-55.6)^2 + (-12)^2]^{1/2} = \pm 56.9$

$\theta = \tan^{-1}\left(\dfrac{R_y}{R_x}\right) = 12.2°$ (in 3rd Quadrant)

So, the resultant force is 56.9 N at 192.2°.

(Force in general)

21. $W = mg$

$m = \dfrac{W}{g} = \dfrac{1150}{9.8} = 117.3$ kg

Mass is the same on Earth and on the Moon. It is 117.3 kg.

The weight on the Moon is,

$W_m = mg_m = 117.3 \times 1.96 = 230$ N

(Force in general)

22. (a) At rest, $F_{fl} = mg = 75 \times 9.8 = 735$ N

F_{fl} = Force exerted by the floor of the elevator.

(b) At constant velocity, there is no extra force involved. So, the force exerted on the floor is the same as in (a).

(c) Net force, $F = F_{fl} - W$

$ma = F_{fl} - mg$

$F_{fl} = ma + mg = m(a+g) = 75(1.3 + 9.8)$

$F_{fl} = 832.5$ N

(d) Net force, $F = F_{fl} - W$

Deceleration means negative acceleration.

$$m(-a) = F_{fl} - mg$$

$$F_{fl} = -ma + mg = m(g-a) = 75(9.8-2)$$

$$F_{fl} = 585 \text{ N}$$

(e) Here, going down decelerating mean acceleration is positive, and the net force,

$$F = F_{fl} - W$$

$$ma = F_{fl} - mg$$

$$F_{fl} = ma + mg = m(a+g) = 75(1.5+9.8)$$

$$F_{fl} = 847.5 \text{ N}$$

(Application of Newton's Laws)

23.

F_A = Applied force

f = Force of friction

The net force on the sled is,

$$F = F_A \cos\theta - f$$

Here, $f = \mu N = \mu(mg - F_A \sin\theta)$

So, $ma = F_A \cos\theta - \mu(mg - F_A \sin\theta)$

Therefore, $a = \dfrac{F_A \cos\theta - \mu(mg - F_A \sin\theta)}{m}$

$$a = \frac{(500)\cos 40° - 0.1 \times 145 \times 9.8 - 500 \sin 40°}{145}$$

$$a = \frac{383 - 110}{145} = 1.88 \text{ m/s}^2$$

(Application of Newton's Laws)

24.

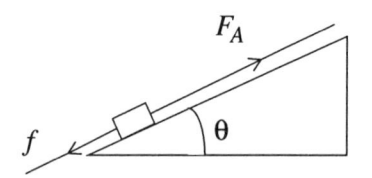

Force of gravity down the plane = $mg\sin\theta$

Force of friction = $f = \mu N = \mu mg\cos\theta$

Applied force = F_A

The net force, $F = F_A - mg\sin\theta - f$

At constant speed, the net force $F = 0$.

$0 = F_A - mg\sin\theta - f$

$F_A = mg\sin\theta + \mu mg\cos\theta$

$ = 25 \times 9.8 \sin 25° + 0.28 \times 25 \times 9.8 \times \cos 25°$

$F_A = 103.5 + 62.2$

$ = 165.7$ N

(Application of Newton's Laws)

25.

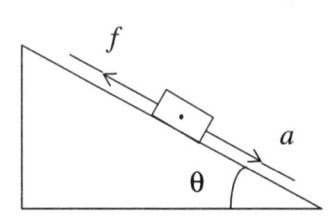

Force of gravity = $mg\sin\theta$

Force of friction = $\mu mg\cos\theta$

The net force, $F = mg\sin\theta - \mu mg\cos\theta$

$ma = mg(\sin\theta - \mu\cos\theta)$

$a = g(\sin\theta - \mu\cos\theta)$

$ = 9.8(\sin 35° - 0.15\cos 35°)$

$ = 9.8(0.574 - 0.123) = 9.8 \times 0.451$

$a = 4.4$ m/s^2

(Application of Newton's Laws)

26. The force of gravity = $W = mg$

The force of friction = $f = \mu mg$

Applied force on the wheels = F_A

The net force, $F = F_A - f$

$$0 = F_A - f$$

$$F_A = f = \mu mg$$

$$ma = \mu mg$$

$$a = \mu g = 0.5 \times 9.8 = 4.9 \, \text{m/s}^2$$

(Force in general)

27.

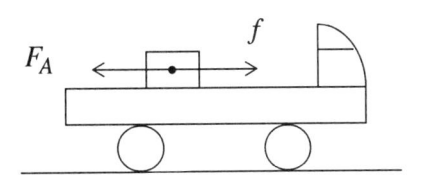

Here, the net force is zero. $F_A = f$

$$ma = \mu mg$$

$$a = \mu g = 0.35 \times 9.8 = 3.43$$

$$a = 3.43 \, \text{m/s}^2$$

(Force in general)

28.

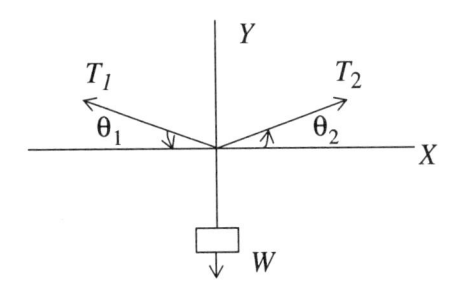

Sum of the forces along the x-axis and y-axis each must be zero, because the net force on the traffic light is zero. For the x component of forces,

$$0 = -T_1 \cos\theta_1 + T_2 \cos\theta_2$$

(x component of T_1 is on the negative x-axis)

$$T_1 \cos 30° - T_2 \cos 40° = 0$$

$$0.866T_1 = 0.766T_2$$

$$T_2 = 1.13T_1$$

And, for y component of forces

$$0 = T_1 \sin\theta_1 + T_2 \sin\theta_2 - W$$

$$0 = T_1 \sin 30° + T_2 \sin 40° - mg$$

$$0 = 0.5T_1 + 0.64T_2 - 65 \times 9.8$$

$$0.5T_1 = 637 - 0.64T_2$$

$$0.5T_1 = 637 - 0.64(1.13T_1) = 637 - 0.723T_1 \text{ (using value of } T_2 \text{ from above)}$$

$$(0.5 + 0.723)T_1 = 637, \quad 1.223T_1 = 637$$

$$T_1 = 520.8 \text{ N}$$

Using value of T_2,

$$T_2 = 1.13T_1 = 1.13 \times 520.8 = 588.6 \text{ N}$$

(Application of Newton's Laws)

29.

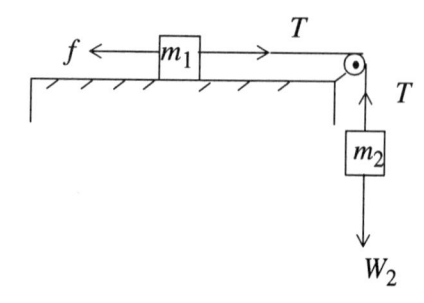

(a) Net force on m_1 is,

$$F = T - f, \, f = 0$$

$$m_1 a = T$$

Net force on m_2 is,

$$F = T - W_2$$

$$m_2(-a) = T - m_2 g, \text{ (acceleration downward)}$$

Using above equation for T,

$$-m_2 a = m_1 a - m_2 g$$

$$a(m_1 + m_2) = m_2 g$$

$$a = \frac{m_2 g}{m_1 + m_2}$$

$$a = \frac{8 \times 9.8}{3 + 8} = 7.1 \, \text{m/s}^2$$

(b) $\qquad\qquad f \neq 0$

Net force on m_1 is, $F = T - f$

$$m_1 a = T - \mu m_1 g$$

$$T = m_1 a + \mu m_1 g$$

Net force on m_2 is,

$$F = T - W_2,$$

again substituting for T gives

$$m_2(-a) = (m_1 a + \mu m_1 g) - m_2 g$$

$$a(m_1 + m_2) = m_2 g - \mu m_1 g$$

$$a = \frac{(m_2 - \mu m_1)}{m_1 + m_2} g$$

$$= \frac{(8 - 0.25 \times 3)(9.8)}{3 + 8}$$

$$a = 6.5 \, \text{m/s}^2$$

(Application of Newton's Laws)

30.

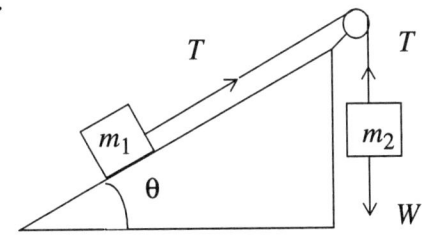

Net force on the mass m_1, along the inclined plane is,

$$F = T - m_1 g \sin\theta$$

$$m_1 a = T - m_1 g \sin\theta$$

$$T = m_1 a + m_1 g \sin\theta$$

Net force on mass m_2 vertically suspended is,

$$F = T - m_2 g$$

$$m_2(-a) = T - m_2 g \quad \text{(Acceleration downward)}$$

Using above expression for T,

$$-m_2 a = (m_1 a + m_1 g \sin\theta) - m_2 g$$

$$(m_1 + m_2)a = m_2 g - m_1 g \sin\theta$$

$$a = \frac{(m_2 - m_1 \sin\theta)g}{m_1 + m_2}, \quad m_1 = m_2$$

$$a = \frac{(1 - \sin\theta)g}{2} = \frac{(1 - \sin 33°)9.8}{2}$$

$$a = 2.2 \text{ m/s}^2$$

(Application of Newton's Laws)

Grade Yourself

Circle the question numbers that you had incorrect. Then indicate the number of questions you missed. If you answered more than three questions incorrectly, you need to focus on that topic. (If a topic has less than three questions and you had at least one wrong, we suggest you study that topic also. Read your textbook, a review book, or ask your teacher for help.)

Subject: Force and Motion

Topic	Question Numbers	Number Incorrect
Force in general	1, 2, 3, 4, 6, 7, 9, 11, 13, 15, 20, 21, 26, 27	
Application of Newton's Laws	5, 8, 10, 12, 14, 16, 17, 18, 19, 22, 23, 24, 25, 28, 29, 30	

Work and Energy

Brief Yourself

Work is done whenever a body moves under the influence of a force.

Work = Force × Distance

Force is a vector and sometimes the direction of the force is different from the direction in which the body moves. In such a situation, one only uses the component of the force which actually does the work. That is:

$W = (F \cos\theta)d$

where W is the work done, F the force applied, d the distance the object moves, and θ the angle between the force and the displacement of the object.

Work being done implies that energy is spent while doing the work. The units of work and energy are the same. Energy associated with motion is called kinetic energy (KE). The ability of an object to do work is related to potential energy (PE). Kinetic energy is given by:

$KE = (1/2)mv^2$ (1)

Here, m stands for mass and v for velocity.

An example of potential energy is the potential energy due to gravity. The potential energy due to gravity may be written as:

$PE = mgh$ (2)

Here, g is the acceleration due to gravity and h stands for the vertical distance of the object above the ground. Another example of potential energy is the energy stored in a compressed or elongated spring. When a mass is attached to one end of a spring while the other end is fixed, the potential energy of the spring is given by:

$PE = (1/2)kx^2$ (3)

where k is the spring constant and x is the amount of compression or elongation of the spring. This relationship comes from Hooke's law.

In many simple situations where the force of friction is not present, the total energy (E) is given by:

$E = KE + PE$ (4)

One of the most important laws of physics is the conservation of energy. In an isolated system, the total energy of the system must be constant.

In some problems, it is of interest to find the rate of doing work which is called power (P). The average power can be stated as:

P = (Work done/Time taken to do the work)

When force and velocity are known in the problem, then power:

P = Force × velocity = Fv

Test Yourself

1. A steady force of 125 N is applied to a shopping cart that moves on a smooth plane parallel to the direction of force. How far does the cart move if 500 J of work are done?

2. A 95 kg person climbs up a 25 m high staircase. How much work is done by the person?

3. A girl does 200 J of work to pull a sled on a smooth horizontal plane with a rope inclined at an angle of 30° with the horizontal (as in the figure below). Find the applied force exerted by the girl if the sled moves a horizontal distance of 5 m.

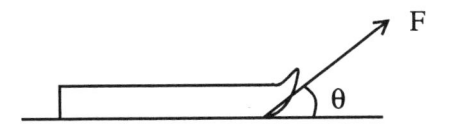

4. A rock at rest falls 30 m vertically down from the edge of a cliff. What is its final speed?

5. A block of mass 5 kg on a smooth horizontal plane is attached to a spring of spring constant 4.5 N/m as in the figure below. It is compressed by 0.25 m and then released. Find the speed of the block when the spring is compressed by 0.15 m.

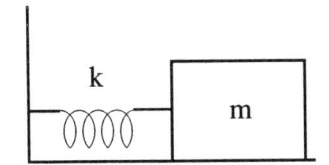

6. A block of mass 7 kg slides down 2 m along a frictionless incline from rest. The angle of the incline is 60° with the horizontal. Find

    (a) the work done by the force of gravity
    (b) the final speed of the block after the 2 m slide.

7. A 1,200 kg car travels at 60 mph. What should the speed of a 55 kg boy be if he wants to have the same kinetic energy as the car?

8. 1,000 J of energy are imparted to a 0.25 kg ball initially at rest. If all of that energy is used to produce kinetic energy of the ball, what is the final speed of the ball?

9. A ball falls freely from rest and strikes the ground 15 m below. What is the speed of the ball as it strikes the ground? Neglect air resistance.

10. A 5 kg box slides down an inclined plane from rest. It falls through a vertical height of 1.5 m. The final speed of the box is 3.5 m/s. How much energy is lost due to forces of friction?

11. An object is thrown upward from the ground with an initial speed of 5 m/s. How far up will the object go? Neglect air resistance.

12. A 4 kg block, sliding at a steady speed of 15 m/s on a frictionless horizontal plane encounters a ramp inclined at 35° with the horizontal. What distance up the ramp will the block move if 20%

of its initial energy is used to overcome friction between the block and the ramp?

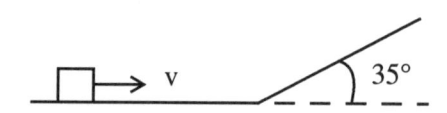

13. A loaded cart is pushed with a horizontal force of 50 N on a frictionless horizontal plane through a distance of 150 m in 20 seconds. What is the power required to do this?

14. A 1,500 watt electric power generator can lift 175 kg of water to a height of 15 m. What is the minimum time in which it can do this?

15. A local electric company charges 9 cents per kilowatt-hour. How much does it cost to run a 1,200 watt washing machine for 45 minutes?

16. The total area of the United States (neglecting Alaska and Hawaii) is 3.5 million square miles; 250 million people live in this region. The average solar energy falling in this area is 180 watts per square meter. Per capita use of electricity is 1,000 watts. Find

    (a) the solar energy falling on this area
    (b) the total area to be covered with solar collectors to satisfy the demand.

17. A child sits in a 5 m long swing suspended at 25° with the vertical. If let go, find the speed of the child at the bottom of the arc.

18. A 0.025 kg ball is shot from a spring gun with a spring constant of 750 N/m. The spring is compressed 0.06 m and the gun is aimed vertically up. How far will the ball rise if fired?

19. A girl in a park starts to slide from rest at the top of a slide 15 m high.

    (a) What is her speed at the bottom of the slide if the incline is frictionless?
    (b) What fraction of total energy is lost to friction if her speed at the bottom is 7 m/s?

20. A rock climber slips from rest and falls 30 m vertically down before her rope straightens out to brake her fall. Find the average deceleration if the rope stretches 3 m to bring her to a stop.

21. A shot-putter pushes a 7.5 kg ball from rest to 15 m/s in 1.8 seconds. Find

    (a) the work done by the shot-putter (ignoring work of gravity)
    (b) the average power to do it.

22. An engine of a jet plane produces a forward thrust of 5,000 lb. What is its horsepower if the plane moves at 600 mph?

23. A flood victim weighing 1300 N is pulled up at a constant speed of 2 m/s by a cable from a rescue helicopter. What is the minimum horsepower of the engine pulling the cable?

24. Two circus clowns each of mass 175 kg swing together with a rope 15 m long starting from rest at an angle of 25°. At the bottom of the arc, one clown steps off. What height above the bottom of arc will the other clown reach?

25. A projectile of mass 10 kg is fired horizontally with a speed of 150 m/s from the edge of a building 200 m high. Find the final kinetic energy of the projectile as it strikes the ground.

26. Water flows over a hydroelectric dam at a rate of 2,500 kg/s. It falls 200 m vertically down before striking the blade of the turbine used to produce electricity. Find the electric power produced if 80% of the energy in the water is converted into electricity.

27. A 2.5 kg block placed on a flat table is attached to the free end of a horizontal spring (k = 215 N/m) while the other end of the spring is fixed as in the figure below. The spring is initially compressed 12 cm and then released. The coefficient of sliding friction is 0.35 between the block and table. What distance will the block move on the table before turning backward?

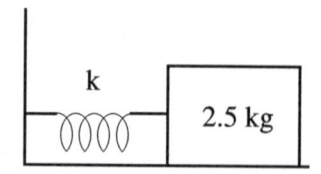

28. How fast should a bicycle rider climb a 45° hill to maintain a power output of 0.33 horsepower? Ignore friction and use 80 kg for the mass of cycle plus rider.

29. A 1,200 kg car has a maximum power output of 15 hp. How steep a ramp can it climb if it maintains a uniform speed of 50 km/hr while the forces of friction add up to 450 N?

30. The annual energy consumption in the United States is 1×10^{20} J. What is the power used in gigawatts?

Check Yourself

1. Work done = Force × Distance

    $500 = 125 \times d$

    $d = \dfrac{500}{125} = 4m$

    (Work)

2. Work done, $W = mgy = 95 \times 9.8 \times 25 = 2.3 \times 10^4$ J

    (Work)

3.

    $W = F(d)\cos\theta$

    $200 = F(5)\cos 30°$

    $F = \dfrac{200}{5(\cos 30°)} = 46.2 N$

    (Work)

4. Initial Energy = $KE + PE = 0 + mgy$

    Final Energy = $KE + PE = \dfrac{1}{2}mv^2 + 0$

    By conservation of energy,

    $mgy = \dfrac{1}{2}mv^2$

    $v^2 = 2gy$

    $v = \sqrt{2gy} = [2 \times 9.8 \times 30]^{1/2} = 24.2$ m/s

    (Conservation of energy)

5. Initial Energy $= KE + PE = 0 + \frac{1}{2}kx_1^2$

Final Energy $= KE + PE = \frac{1}{2}mv^2 + \frac{1}{2}kx_2^2$

conservation of energy means,

$$\frac{1}{2}kx_1^2 = \frac{1}{2}mv^2 + \frac{1}{2}kx_2^2$$

$$\frac{1}{2}mv^2 = \frac{1}{2}k(x_1^2 - x_2^2)$$

$$v^2 = \frac{k}{m}(x_1^2 - x_2^2)$$

$$v = \sqrt{\frac{k}{m}(x_1^2 - x_2^2)}$$

$$= \left[\frac{4.5}{5}(0.25^2 - 0.15^2)\right]^{1/2}$$

$$= [0.9(0.0625 - 0.0225)]^{1/2}$$

$$= 0.19 \text{ m/s}$$

(Conservation of energy)

6. (a) Force of gravity down the incline $= (mg\sin\theta)$

Work done $= (mg\sin\theta)d$

$= 7 \times 9.8 \times \sin 60° \times 2$

$= 119$ J

(b) Work done = change in kinetic energy

$$mg(\sin\theta)d = \frac{1}{2}mv^2 - 0$$

$$v^2 = 2g(\sin\theta)d$$

$$v = \sqrt{2gd\sin\theta} = [2 \times 9.8 \times 2 \times \sin 60°]^{1/2}$$

$$v = 5.8 \text{ m/s}$$

(Work)

7. KE of car $= \frac{1}{2}m_1 v_1^2$

KE of boy $= \frac{1}{2}m_2 v_2^2$

$$\frac{1}{2}m_1v_1^2 = \frac{1}{2}m_2v_2^2$$

$$v_2^2 = \frac{m_1v_1^2}{m_2}$$

$$v_2 = \left[\frac{m_1v_1^2}{m_2}\right]^{1/2} = \left[\frac{1200 \times 60^2}{55}\right]^{1/2} = 280 \text{ mph}$$

(Work)

8. $$W = \frac{1}{2}mv^2$$

$$1000 = \frac{1}{2} \times 0.25 \times v^2$$

$$v = \sqrt{\frac{2 \times 1000}{0.25}} = 89.4 \text{ m/s}$$

(Conservation of energy)

9. Initial Energy $= KE + PE = 0 + mgy$

Final Energy $= KE + PE = \frac{1}{2}mv^2 + 0$

By conservation of energy,

$$mgy = \frac{1}{2}mv^2$$

$$v^2 = 2gy$$

$$v = \sqrt{2gy} = [2 \times 9.8 \times 15]^{1/2}$$

$$v = 17.1 \text{ m/s}$$

(Conservation of energy)

10. We begin by calculating the final speed assuming no loss of energy to friction:

Initial Energy $= KE + PE = 0 + mgy_1$

Final Energy $= KE + PE = \frac{1}{2}mv^2 + mgy_2$

$$mgy_1 = \frac{1}{2}mv^2 + mgy_2$$

$$v^2 = 2g(y_1 - y_2)$$

$$v = \sqrt{2g(y_1 - y_2)}$$

84 / Physics I

$$v = [2 \times 9.8(1.5)]^{1/2} = 5.4 \text{ m/s}$$

Energy loss to friction = Difference of KE

$$= \frac{1}{2}mv_2^2 - \frac{1}{2}mv_1^2,$$

where v_2 = final speed if no friction is present,

and v_1 = final speed with friction present

$$= \frac{1}{2}m(v_2^2 - v_1^2)$$

$$= \frac{1}{2} \times 5(5.4^2 - 3.5^2)$$

$$= 42.3 \text{ J}$$

(Conservation of energy)

11. Initial Energy = $KE + PE = \frac{1}{2}mv^2 + 0$

    Final Energy = $KE + PE = 0 + mgy$

    $$\frac{1}{2}mv^2 = mgy$$

    $$v^2 = 2gy$$

    $$y = \frac{v^2}{2g} = \frac{5^2}{2 \times 9.8} = 1.3 \text{ m}$$

(Conservation of energy)

12. Initial Energy = $KE + PE = \frac{1}{2}mv^2 + 0$

    $$= \frac{1}{2} \times 4 \times 15^2 = 450 \text{ J}$$

    Final Energy = $KE + PE$ + Friction energy

    $$= 0 + mgy + 20\% \text{ of Initial energy}$$

    By conservation of energy,

    $$450 = 4 \times 9.8 \times y + 450 \times 0.2$$

    $$y = \frac{450 - 90}{4 \times 9.8} = 9.2 \text{ m}$$

    $$\sin\theta = \frac{y}{r}, \quad r = \frac{y}{\sin\theta}$$

$$r = \frac{9.2}{\sin 35°} = 16.0 \text{ m}$$

Block will rise 16 m along the ramp.

(Conservation of energy)

13. $$\text{Power} = \frac{\text{Work done}}{\text{Time}} = \frac{50 \times 150}{20}$$

$$P = 375 \text{ watts}$$

(Power)

14. $$P = 1500 \text{ watts}$$

Work done = $W = mgy = 175 \times 9.8 \times 15 =$

$$W = 2.57 \times 10^4 \text{ J}$$

$$P = \frac{W}{t}, \quad t = \frac{W}{P} = \frac{2.57 \times 10^4}{1,500}$$

$$t = 17.1 \text{ s}$$

(Power)

15. Kilowatt hours used

$$= \frac{1,200}{1,000} \times \frac{45}{60} = 0.9 \text{ kilowatt hour}$$

Cost = $0.09 \times 0.9 = $0.08 = 8 ¢

(Power)

16. (a) Solar energy per unit area = 180 w/m²

$$\text{Total area} = 3.5 \times 10^6 \times 2.59 \times 10^6 = 9.1 \times 10^{12} \text{ m}^2$$

Total solar energy/unit time = $180 \times 9.1 \times 10^{12}$

$$= 1.6 \times 10^{15} \text{ W}$$

(b) Per capita use = 1,000 W

$$\text{Total use} = 1,000 \times 250 \times 10^6 = 2.5 \times 10^{11} \text{ W}$$

Total area of solar collectors needed

$$= \frac{2.5 \times 10^{11}}{180} = 1.4 \times 10^9 \text{ m}^2$$

(Power)

17.

Initial Energy $= KE + PE = 0 + mgy_1$

Final Energy $= KE + PE = \dfrac{1}{2}mv^2 + mgy_2$

By conservation of energy,

$$mgy_1 = \dfrac{1}{2}mv^2 + mgy_2$$

$$v^2 = 2g(y_1 - y_2)$$

$$v = \sqrt{2g(y_1 - y_2)}$$

$(y_1 - y_2) = L(1 - \cos\theta)$

$\qquad = 5(1 - \cos 25°)$

$\qquad = 0.47$ m

$v = [2 \times 9.8 \times 0.47]^{1/2} = 3$ m/s

(Conservation of energy)

18. PE of the spring $= \dfrac{1}{2}kx^2$

By conservation of energy,

$$\dfrac{1}{2}kx^2 = mgy$$

$$y = \dfrac{kx^2}{2mg} = \dfrac{750 \times 0.06^2}{2 \times 0.025 \times 9.8}$$

$y = 5.5$ m

(Conservation of energy)

19. (a) $\dfrac{1}{2}mv^2 = mgy$

$\qquad v^2 = 2gy$

$\qquad v = \sqrt{2gy} = [2 \times 9.8 \times 15]^{1/2} = 17.1$ m/s

(b)   Energy without friction = $\frac{1}{2}mv_1^2$

Energy in presence of friction = $\frac{1}{2}mv_2^2$

Difference = $\frac{1}{2}m(v_1^2 - v_2^2)$

Percent lost to friction = $\dfrac{\frac{1}{2}m(v_1^2 - v_2^2)}{\frac{1}{2}mv_1^2} \times 100$

$= \dfrac{v_1^2 - v_2^2}{v_1^2} \times 100 = \dfrac{17.1^2 - 7^2}{17.1^2} \times 100$

$= 83\%$

(Conservation of energy)

20. $\frac{1}{2}mv_0^2 = mgy$

$v_0 = \sqrt{2gy} = [2 \times 9.8 \times 30]^{1/2} = 24.2$ m/s

$v^2 = v_0^2 + 2ay$

$0 = 24.2^2 + 2(a)3$

$a = -\dfrac{24.2^2}{2 \times 3} = -98$ m/s^2

(Conservation of energy)

21. (a) Work done, W = Change in Kinetic Energy

$= \frac{1}{2}mv^2 - 0 = \frac{1}{2} \times 7.5 \times 15^2 = 843.7$ J

(b) Power = $\dfrac{843.7}{1.8} = 468.7$ watts

(Power)

22.   Force of thrust = 5000 lbs = 5000×4.45 N

$= 22250$ N

$v = 600$ mph = 600×0.447 m/s = 268 m/s

Power, $P = Fv = 22250 \times 268$

$P = 6 \times 10^6$ watts = 8000 hp

(Power)

23. Power, $P = Fv = 1300 \times 2 = 2600$ watts

    = 3.5 hp

(Power)

24. Initial Energy = $0 + (2m)gy_1$

    Energy at bottom of arc before one of them steps off = $(2m)gy_2 + KE$

    KE at bottom of arc before one of them steps off = $(2m)g(y_1 - y_2)$

    $(y_1 - y_2) = L(1 - \cos\theta) = 15(1 - \cos 25°)$

    = 1.4 m

    Therefore, energy before one of them steps off = KE of the two at bottom of the arc = $(2m)g(y_1 - y_2) = 2 \times 175 \times 9.8 \times 1.4 = 4802$ J

    Because, the other clown takes away half of the energy.

    So, final energy = $mg(y_3 - y_2) = 2401$ J

    Therefore, $(y_3 - y_2) = \dfrac{2401}{mg} = \dfrac{2401}{175 \times 9.8} = 1.4$ m

(Conservation of energy)

25. $v_x = 150$ m/s = constant

    $v_y = \sqrt{2gy} = [2 \times 9.8 \times 200]^{1/2} = 62.6$ m/s

    $v = \sqrt{150^2 + 62.6^2} = 162.5$ m/s

    Final $KE = \dfrac{1}{2}mv^2 = \dfrac{1}{2} \times 10 \times 162.5^2$

    = 1.32×10^5 J

(Conservation of energy)

26. $v = \sqrt{2gy} = [2 \times 9.8 \times 200]^{1/2} = \sqrt{3,920} = 62.6$ m/s

    $KE = \dfrac{1}{2}mv^2$

    Power = $\dfrac{\frac{1}{2}mv^2}{t} = \dfrac{1}{2}\left(\dfrac{m}{t}\right)v^2 = \dfrac{1}{2} \times (2,500)62.6^2 = 4.9 \times 10^6$ w

Electric Power = $P \times 0.8 = 4.9 \times 10^6 \times 0.8$

$= 3.9 \times 10^6$ watts

(Power)

27.

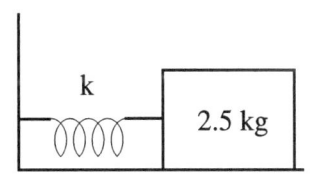

Energy stored in the spring = $\frac{1}{2}kx_0^2 = \frac{1}{2} \times 215 \times 0.12^2 = 1.55$ J

Force of friction = $\mu N = \mu mg = 0.35 \times 2.5 \times 9.8$

$f = 8.57$ N

Work done against friction coming to relaxed position = $fx = 8.57 \times 0.12 = 1.0$ J

Energy remaining at relaxed position = $1.55 - 1.0 = 0.55$ J

Let the spring continue to elongate distance x_1 beyond the relaxed position before coming momentarily to rest at maximum extension.

Energy loss during this time = $fx_1 = 8.57 x_1$

Potential energy of elongation = $\frac{1}{2}kx_1^2 = \frac{1}{2} \times 215 \times (x_1)^2 = 107.5 x_1^2$

By conservation of energy,

$107.5 x_1^2 + 8.57 x_1 = 0.55$

$107.5 x_1^2 + 8.57 x_1 - 0.55 = 0$

$x_1 = \frac{-8.57}{2 \times 107.5} \pm \frac{\sqrt{8.57^2 + 4(107.5)(0.55)}}{2 \times 107.5}$

$= -0.04 \pm 0.08$

$x_1 = 0.04$ m

Total distance block moves = $0.12 + 0.04 = 0.16$ m

(Conservation of energy)

28. Power = P = 0.33 hp = 0.33 × 746 = 246 watts

    $P = Fv$

    $P = (mg\sin\theta)v$

    $246 = 80 \times 9.8 \times (\sin 45°)v = 554.4v$

    $v = \dfrac{246}{554.4} = 0.444$ m/s = 44.4 cm/s

    (Power)

29. $v = 50$ km/hr $= \dfrac{50 \times 10^3}{60 \times 60} = 13.9$ m/s

    $P = 15$ hp $= 15 \times 746 = 11{,}190$ watts

    $P = Fv$

    Net force in presence of friction = $mg\sin\theta + f$

    $P = (mg\sin\theta + f)v$

    $11{,}190 = (1{,}200 \times 9.8 \times \sin\theta + 450)13.9$

    $805 = 1{,}200 \times 9.8\sin\theta + 450$

    $355 = 11{,}760\sin\theta$

    $\sin\theta = 0.03$

    $\theta = 1.7°$

    (Power)

30. $P = \dfrac{\text{Work done}}{\text{Time}} = \dfrac{1 \times 10^{20} \text{ J}}{365 \text{ days}}$

    $P = \dfrac{1 \times 10^{20}}{365 \times 24 \times 60 \times 60}$ W

    $P = 3.171 \times 10^{12}$ W

    $P = 3{,}171$ gigawatts

    (Power)

Grade Yourself

Circle the question numbers that you had incorrect. Then indicate the number of questions you missed. If you answered more than three questions incorrectly, you need to focus on that topic. (If a topic has less than three questions and you had at least one wrong, we suggest you study that topic also. Read your textbook, a review book, or ask your teacher for help.)

Subject: Work and Energy

Topic	Question Numbers	Number Incorrect
Work	1, 2, 3, 6, 7	
Conservation of energy	4, 5, 8, 9, 10, 11, 12, 17, 18, 19, 20, 24, 25, 27	
Power	13, 14, 15, 16, 21, 22, 23, 26, 28, 29, 30	

Momentum and Impulse

7

Brief Yourself

When an object moves, its amount of motion is measured with a basic quantity called momentum. Momentum is a vector quantity. It is closely related to the concept of force. Many problems involving collisions are solved by the principle of conservation of momentum.

The linear momentum of a body is defined as:

$$\mathbf{p} = m\mathbf{v} \tag{1}$$

Where $\mathbf{p}$ is the linear momentum of the body, m is mass and $\mathbf{v}$ is the velocity of the body.

Force $\mathbf{F}$ can be defined as:

$$\mathbf{F} = \frac{\Delta p}{\Delta t}$$

Where change of momentum $\Delta p = \mathbf{p}_f - \mathbf{p}_i$

and change in time $\Delta t = t_f - t_i$

In many problems such as collisions, the time t during which force acts is small. A quantity called impulse is a useful measure and it is defined as:

$$\text{Impulse} = \mathbf{p}_f - \mathbf{p}_i = \mathbf{F}t \tag{2}$$

Conservation of linear momentum can be stated as:

Initial momentum = Final momentum

In one dimensional collision problems between two bodies:

$$m_1 v_{1i} + m_2 v_{2i} = m_1 v_{1f} + m_2 v_{2f} \tag{3}$$

In two dimensional collision problems, the conservation law of linear momentum applies along both the x-axis and the y-axis.

In the case of an elastic collision, the total kinetic energy is also conserved. When bodies suffer inelastic collisions, the total kinetic energy is *not* conserved. Linear momentum, however, is *always* conserved without regard to the collisions being elastic or inelastic.

Test Yourself

1. A baseball of mass 0.2 kg is thrown at a horizontal speed of 20 m/s. If its speed is doubled, find the ratio of momenta and kinetic energies for the two cases.

2. A ball of mass 1.0 kg moving to the left at a speed of 25 m/s suffers an elastic collision with a fixed vertical wall and comes backward with the same speed.

   (a) Find the impulse of the ball.
   (b) Find the force suffered by the wall if the ball remains in contact with the wall for 0.15 sec.

3. A 10 kg body, initially at rest, explodes suddenly into two pieces of mass 4 kg and 6 kg. Find the velocity of the 4 kg mass if the other moves east at 25 m/s.

4. A billiard ball of mass 0.2 kg moving at 15 m/s suffers a head on elastic collision with an identical billiard ball at rest. What are the kinetic energies and momenta of the two balls after collision?

5. A 50 kg ballet dancer makes a leap to the left at a speed of 5 m/s on to the arms of her partner at rest. The male dancer exerts a steady horizontal force of 350 N while catching his partner to a stop. What is the time to reduce her momentum to zero?

6. A firefighter uses his hose to spray water onto the wall of a burning building. The water strikes the wall horizontally at a rate of 25 kg/s and with a speed of 5 m/s before coming to stop on the wall. Find the magnitude of the average force exerted on the wall by the gushing water.

7. An empty railway car of mass 15,000 kg is coasting at 3.5 m/s on a level track. A load of 5,000 kg of coal is dropped into the car from above at zero horizontal speed from above. Find the new velocity of the car plus coal.

8. A ball of mass 1.5 kg moving at 5.5 m/s strikes a second ball of mass 4.0 kg (at rest) in a head on elastic collision. What are the final speeds of the two balls?

9. A 0.09 kg bullet is fired horizontally into an 8 kg block of wood at rest on a frictionless plane. The block of wood now containing the bullet moves at a steady speed of 0.5 m/s after the impact. Find the initial velocity of the bullet.

10. An aggressive heavyweight boxer throws a horizontal 1.0 megawatt punch at 150 m/s that lands on the face of his opponent at rest. The punch comes to a halt in 0.2 sec. Find the force and impulse experienced by his opponent.

11. A baseball player strikes a 0.25 kg ball moving at 15 m/s and sends it backward with a velocity of 25 m/s. The ball is in contact with the bat for 0.05 sec. Find the magnitude of the impulse and the average force on the ball exerted by the batter.

12. A glider of mass 0.75 kg moves right on a frictionless air track at 4.0 m/s and collides head-on with a second glider of mass 0.15 kg moving left at 8.0 m/s. Find the final velocities of the two gliders if the collision is perfectly elastic.

13. A 500 kg gun fires a 1.5 kg shell with a muzzle velocity of 650 m/s.

    (a) Find the recoil velocity of the gun.
    (b) If the recoil is opposite a resistive force of 1,600 N, find the time in which the gun is brought to rest.

14. A 0.45 kg ball moving at 5.0 m/s collides head-on with another ball of mass 0.15 kg moving at 22 m/s in the opposite direction. Find the velocity of each if the collision is perfectly inelastic (i.e., the balls remain stuck together).

15. At a road intersection, a car moving north at 20 m/s collides with another car of identical mass moving east at 15 m/s. Find the speed and direction of the wreckage if the two cars remain tangled after the collision.

16. A 0.125 kg bullet is fired horizontally into an 8 kg block of wood which is vertically suspended by a long rope. The block rises a vertical distance of 15 cm from its initial position of rest with the bullet embedded in it (see the following figure).

Find the initial speed of the bullet.

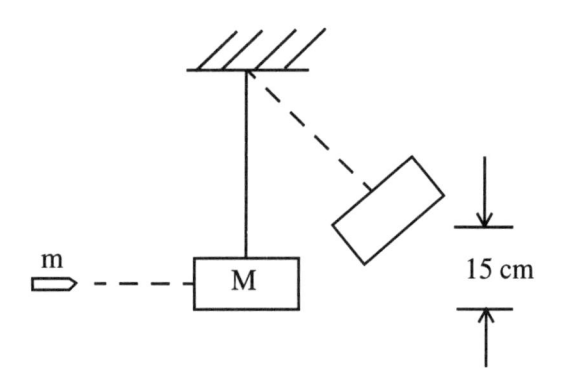

17. A 1.5 kg ball moving forward strikes a second ball of mass 2.5 kg in a head-on perfectly elastic collision. The second ball, initially moving forward at a speed of 0.25 m/s, changes its forward speed to 0.75 m/s after the collision. Find the velocities of the first ball before and after the collision.

18. An ice skater of mass 80 kg moving east at 8 m/s collides with a second ice skater of mass 75 kg moving north at an unknown speed on a frictionless horizontal surface. After the collision the two skaters stick together and move at an angle of 30° north of east. Find the unknown speed of the second skater and the speed of the two after the collision.

19. In a Hollywood movie, Tarzan, of mass 85 kg, swings from a 3 m vine which is horizontal at the start. At the bottom of the arc in his swing downward, he picks up Jane, of mass 55 kg, in a perfectly inelastic collision. What maximum height of a tree limb can they reach on the upward swing?

20. An 11 kg rock at rest at the origin of coordinates suddenly explodes into three pieces of mass 2.0 kg, 3.5 kg, and 5.5 kg. The 2.0 kg mass moves east at 4.0 m/s and the 5.5 kg mass moves south at 2.0 m/s. Find the speed and direction of the 3.5 kg mass.

21. A metal puck on a frictionless horizontal table moves at a speed of 6.5 m/s along the x-axis. It makes a glancing elastic collision with an identical stationary puck. After the collision, the first puck moves off at a speed of 3.5 m/s along a direction north of x-axis. Find the speed and direction of the second puck after the collision.

22. A block of mass 10 kg starts to move at 12 m/s on a rough road. It moves 1.5 meters before suffering a head-on elastic collision with a block of mass 20 kg at rest. The coefficient of friction is 0.3 between the road and the blocks.

    (a) Find the final velocities just after the collision.
    (b) Find the displacement of the first and the second block upon coming to rest.

23. A shell is fired from a mortar with an initial speed of 250 m/s at an angle of 40° with respect to the ground. Unfortunately, it explodes in midair before reaching the target on the ground. Where will the center of mass among all the fragments reach the ground?

Check Yourself

1. $p_1 = m_1 v_1 = 0.2 \times 20 = 4 \text{ kg} \cdot \text{m/s}$

    $p_2 = m_2 v_2 = 0.2 \times 40 = 8 \text{ kg} \cdot \text{m/s}$

    $\dfrac{p_2}{p_1} = \dfrac{8}{4} = 2$

    $KE_1 = \dfrac{1}{2} m_1 v_1^2 = \dfrac{1}{2} \times 0.2 \times 20^2 = 40 \text{ J}$

$KE_2 = \frac{1}{2}m_2v_2^2 = \frac{1}{2} \times 0.2 \times 40^2 = 160$ J

$\dfrac{KE_2}{KE_1} = \dfrac{160}{40} = 4$

Ratio = 4

(Impulse/momentum)

2. (a) Impulse = $p_f - p_i = 1 \times 25 - 1 \times (-25)$

$= 25 + 25 = 50$

Impulse = 50 kg · m/s

(b) Impulse = $(F)(t)$

$50 = (F) \, 0.15$

$F = \dfrac{50}{0.15} = 333$ N

$F = 333$ N to the left

(Impulse/momentum)

3. Initial momentum = Final momentum

$0 = m_1v_1 + m_2v_2$

$m_2v_2 = -m_1v_1$

$v_2 = -\dfrac{m_1v_1}{m_2} = -\dfrac{6}{4} \times 25 = -37.5$

$v_2 = -37.5$ m/s

4 kg mass moves west at 37.5 m/s.

(Inelastic collision)

4. From conservation of momentum

$m_1v_{1i} + m_2v_{2i} = m_1v_{1f} + m_2v_{2f}$

Here, $m_1 = m_2$ and $v_{2i} = 0$

$v_{1i} + 0 = v_{1f} + v_{2f}$

$v_{1i} = v_{1f} + v_{2f}$ \hfill (1)

From conservation of kinetic energy,

$$\frac{1}{2}m_1 v_{1i}^2 = \frac{1}{2}m_1 v_{1f}^2 + \frac{1}{2}m_2 v_{2f}^2$$

$$v_{1i}^2 = v_{1f}^2 + v_{2f}^2$$

Using equation (1),

$$(v_{1f} + v_{2f})^2 = v_{1f}^2 + v_{2f}^2$$

$$v_{1f}^2 + 2v_{1f}v_{2f} + v_{2f}^2 = v_{1f}^2 + v_{2f}^2$$

$$v_{1f}v_{2f} = 0 \qquad (2)$$

If the product of the two is zero, then one or both of them are zero.

From conservation of momentum, both v_{1f} and v_{2f} cannot be zero. So, one of them is zero. Here v_{1f} is zero.

So, $v_{1i} = v_{2f}$

The ball initially at rest moves at 15 m/s. The ball initially moving at 15 m/s stops after collision. Momenta are,

$$m_1 v_{1i} = m_2 v_{2f} = 0.2 \times 15 = 3$$

$$m_1 v_{1f} = 0 \qquad m_2 v_{2f} = 3.0 \text{ kg} \cdot \text{m/s}$$

Final kinetic energies are given by,

$$\frac{1}{2}m_1 v_{1i}^2 = \frac{1}{2}m_2 v_{2f}^2 = \frac{1}{2} \times 0.2 \times 15^2 = 22.5$$

$(KE)_2 = 22.5 \text{ J}$, $(KE)_1 = 0$

(Elastic collision)

5. Impulse $= (F)(t) = p_f - p_i$

$$350(t) = 0 - (50)(-5)$$

$$t = \frac{50 \times 5}{350} = 0.71, t = 0.71 \text{ s}$$

(Impulse/momentum)

6. Impulse,

$$(F)(t) = p_f - p_i = 0 - p_i$$

$$F = -\frac{p_i}{t} = -\frac{mv_i}{t} = -\left(\frac{m}{t}\right)v_i$$

$$|F| = (25)5 = 125$$

$|F| = 125$ N

(Impulse/momentum)

7. Initial momentum = Final momentum

$$m_1 v_1 = m_2 v_2$$

$$(15000)3.5 = (15000 + 5000)v_2$$

$$v_2 = \frac{15}{20} \times 3.5 = 2.6, \quad v_2 = 2.6 \text{ m/s}$$

(Inelastic collision)

8. From conservation of momentum

$$m_1 v_{1i} + m_2 v_{2i} = m_1 v_{1f} + m_2 v_{2f}$$

$$(1.5)(5.5) + 0 = 1.5 v_{1f} + (4) v_{2f}$$

$$8.25 = 1.5 v_{1f} + (4) v_{2f} \tag{1}$$

$$v_{2f} = 2.06 - 0.375 v_{1f} \tag{2}$$

From conservation of kinetic energy

$$\frac{1}{2} m_1 v_{1i}^2 + \frac{1}{2} m_2 v_{2i}^2 = \frac{1}{2} m_1 v_{1f}^2 + \frac{1}{2} m_2 v_{2f}^2$$

$$m_1 v_{1i}^2 + 0 = m_1 v_{1f}^2 + m_2 v_{2f}^2$$

Substituting from equation (2)

$$(1.5)(5.5)^2 = (1.5) v_{1f}^2 + 4(2.06 - 0.375 v_{1f})^2$$

$$45.4 = 1.5 v_{1f}^2 + 4(4.24 - 1.54 v_{1f} + 0.14 v_{1f}^2)$$

$$45.4 = 1.5 v_{1f}^2 + 17 - 6.16 v_{1f} + 0.56 v_{1f}^2$$

$$2.06 v_{1f}^2 - 6.16 v_{1f} - 28.4 = 0$$

$$v_{1f} = \frac{6.16}{4.12} \pm \frac{\sqrt{6.16^2 + 4(2.06)(28.4)}}{4.12}$$

$$= 1.49 \pm \frac{16.5}{4.12}$$

$$= 1.49 \pm 4$$

$$v_{1f} = 5.5 \text{ or } -2.5,$$

From equation (2),

$v_{2f} = 2.06 - 0.375(5.5) = 0$

or

$2.06 - 0.375(-2.5) = 3$

From equation (1),

momentum is conserved only if,

$v_{1f} = -2.5$ m/s and $v_{2f} = 3$ m/s

(Elastic collision)

9. From conservation of momentum,

$$m_1 v_{1i} + m_2 v_{2i} = (m_1 + m_2) v_f$$

$$m_1 v_{1i} + 0 = (m_1 + m_2) v_f$$

$$0.09 \, v_{1i} = (0.09 + 8) 0.5$$

$$0.09 \, v_{1i} = 4.04$$

$$v_{1i} = 45 \text{ m/s}$$

(Inelastic collision)

10. Power, $P = Fv$

$$1 \times 10^6 = F(150)$$

$$F = 6.7 \times 10^3 \text{ N}$$

Impulse $= (F)(t) = (6.7 \times 10^3)(0.2) = 1.3 \times 10^3$

Impulse $= 1.3 \times 10^3$ N · s

(Impulse/momentum)

11. Impulse $= p_f - p_i = (0.25)25 - (0.25)(-15)$

$= 6.25 + 3.75 = 10$ kg · m/s

Impulse $= (F)(t)$

$10 = (F)(0.05)$

$F = 200$ N

(Impulse/momentum)

12. From conservation of momentum

$$m_1 v_{1i} + m_2 v_{2i} = m_1 v_{1f} + m_2 v_{2f}$$

$$0.75(4) + (0.15)(-8) = 0.75v_{1f} + 0.15v_{2f}$$

$$3 - 1.2 = 0.75v_{1f} + 0.15v_{2f}$$

$$v_{1f} = 2.4 - 0.2v_{2f} \qquad (1)$$

From conservation of kinetic energy,

$$\frac{1}{2}m_1v_{1i}^2 + \frac{1}{2}m_2v_{2i}^2 = \frac{1}{2}m_1v_{1f}^2 + \frac{1}{2}m_2v_{2f}^2$$

$$(0.75)(4)^2 + (0.15)8^2 = 0.75v_{1f}^2 + 0.15v_{2f}^2$$

$$21.6 = 0.75(2.4 - 0.2v_{2f})^2 + 0.15v_{2f}^2 \text{ using equation (1).}$$

$$21.6 = 0.75(5.76 - 0.96v_{2f} + 0.04v_{2f}^2) + 0.15v_{2f}^2$$

$$21.6 = 4.32 - 0.72v_{2f} + 0.03v_{2f}^2 + 0.15v_{2f}^2$$

$$0.18v_{2f}^2 - 0.72v_{2f} - 17.28 = 0$$

$$v_{2f}^2 - 4v_{2f} - 96 = 0$$

$$v_{2f} = \frac{4}{2} \pm \frac{\sqrt{4^2 + 4(96)}}{2} = 2 \pm 10$$

$$v_{2f} = -8 \text{ or } 10$$

And from equation (1), $v_{1f} = 4$ m/s if $v_{2f} = -8$ m/s, or (2)

$v_{1f} = 0.4$ m/s if $v_{2f} = 10$ m/s

Equation (2) is impossible since the gliders cannot retain their initial velocities

Therefore, $v_{1f} = 0.4$ m/s

$$v_{2f} = 10 \text{ m/s}$$

(Elastic collision)

13. (a) From conservation of momentum,

$$m_1v_{1i} + m_2v_{2i} = m_1v_{1f} + m_2v_{2f}$$

$$0 + 0 = (1.5)(650) + (500)v_{2f} = 972 + 500v_{2f}$$

$$v_{2f} = -1.95 \text{ m/s}$$

(b) Impulse $= p_f - p_i = (F)(t)$

$$(-1.95)(500) - 0 = (-1600)t$$

$1600t = 975, \quad t = 0.6s$

(Impulse/momentum)

14. Momentum must be conserved. A perfectly inelastic collision implies $v_{1f} = v_{2f}$.

$$m_1 v_{1i} + m_2 v_{2i} = (m_1 + m_2) v_f$$

$$(0.45)(5) + (0.15)(-22) = (0.45 + 0.15) v_f$$

$$2.25 - 3.3 = 0.6 v_f$$

$$v_f = -1.75 \text{ m/s}$$

Both stick together and move at 1.75 m/s in opposite direction.

(Inelastic collision)

15.

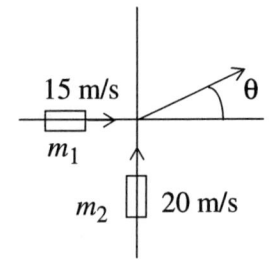

From conservation of momentum in two dimensions,

along x-axis: $m_1 v_1 = (m_1 + m_2) v_f \cos\theta$

Since $m_1 = m_2$,

$$v_1 = 2 v_f \cos\theta$$

$$15 = 2 v_f \cos\theta$$

$$v_f \cos\theta = 7.5 \qquad (1)$$

along y-axis:

$$m_2 v_2 = (m_1 + m_2) v_f \sin\theta, \quad m_1 = m_2$$

$$v_2 = 2 v_f \sin\theta$$

$$20 = 2 v_f \sin\theta$$

$$v_f \sin\theta = 10 \qquad (2)$$

$$\frac{v_f \sin\theta}{v_f \cos\theta} = \frac{10}{7.5} = 1.33$$

$$\tan\theta = 1.33$$

$$\theta = 53.1°$$

From (1), $v_f \cos\theta = 7.5$

$$v_f = \frac{7.5}{\cos\theta} = \frac{7.5}{\cos 53.1°}, \quad v_f = 12.5 \text{ m/s}$$

(Inelastic collision)

16. From conservation of energy,

    KE of (block + bullet = PE of height

    $$\frac{1}{2}(m + Mv_f^2) = (m + M)gy$$

    $$v_f^2 = 2gy$$

    From conservation of momentum,

    $$mv_i = (m + M)v_f$$

    $$v_i = \frac{(m + M)\sqrt{2gy}}{m}$$

    $$= \frac{(0.125 + 8)\sqrt{2(9.8)(0.15)}}{0.125}$$

    $$v_i = 111 \text{ m/s}$$

(Inelastic collision)

17. From conservation of momentum

    $$m_1 v_{1i} + m_2 v_{2i} = m_1 v_{1f} + m_2 v_{2f} \quad (1)$$

    $$m_1(v_{1i} - v_{1f}) = m_2(v_{2f} - v_{2i}) \quad (2)$$

    From conservation of KE,

    $$\frac{1}{2}m_1 v_{1i}^2 + \frac{1}{2}m_2 v_{2i}^2 = \frac{1}{2}m_1 v_{1f}^2 + \frac{1}{2}m_2 v_{2f}^2$$

    $$m_1(v_{1i}^2 - v_{1f}^2) = m_2(v_{2f}^2 - v_{2i}^2)$$

    $$m_1(v_{1i} - v_{1f})(v_{1i} + v_{1f}) = m_2(v_{2f} - v_{2i})(v_{2f} + v_{2i})$$

    Using equation (2),

$$v_{1i} + v_{1f} = v_{2f} + v_{2i}$$

Therefore, $v_{2f} = v_{1i} - v_{2i} + v_{1f}$ \hfill (3)

Using the value of v_{2f} from equation (3) in equation (1),

$$m_1 v_{1i} + m_2 v_{2i} = m_1 v_{1f} + m_2(v_{1i} - v_{2i} + v_{1f})$$

$$m_1 v_{1i} + m_2 v_{2i} = m_1 v_{1f} + m_2 v_{1i} - m_2 v_{2i} + m_2 v_{1f}$$

$$v_{1f}(m_1 + m_2) = v_{1i}(m_1 - m_2) + 2m_2 v_{2i}$$

$$v_{1f} = \frac{2m_2}{m_1 + m_2} v_{2i} + \left(\frac{m_1 - m_2}{m_1 + m_2}\right) v_{1i} \tag{4}$$

Using (4) in equation (3) we get,

$$v_{2f} = v_{1i} - v_{2i} + \left(\frac{2m_2}{m_1 + m_2} v_{2i} + \frac{m_1 - m_2}{m_1 + m_2} v_{1i}\right)$$

$$v_{2f} = \left(1 + \frac{m_1 - m_2}{m_1 + m_2}\right) v_{1i} - \left(1 - \frac{2m_2}{m_1 + m_2}\right) v_{2i}$$

$$v_{2f} = \frac{2m_1}{m_1 + m_2} v_{1i} - \left(\frac{m_1 - m_2}{m_1 + m_2}\right) v_{2i} \tag{5}$$

From equation (5),

$$0.75 = \frac{2 \cdot 1.5}{1.5 + 2.5} v_{1i} - \left(\frac{1.5 - 2.5}{1.5 + 2.5}\right)(0.25)$$

$$0.75 = 0.75 v_{1i} + 0.0625$$

$$v_{1i} = 0.92 \text{ m/s}$$

Using equation (4),

$$v_{1f} = \frac{2 \times 2.5}{1.5 + 2.5}(0.25) + \left(\frac{1.5 - 2.5}{1.5 + 2.5}\right) 0.92$$

$$= \frac{5}{4}(0.25) + \frac{(-1)(0.92)}{4} = 0.31 - 0.23 = 0.08$$

$$v_{1f} = 0.08 \text{ m/s}$$

(Elastic collision)

18.

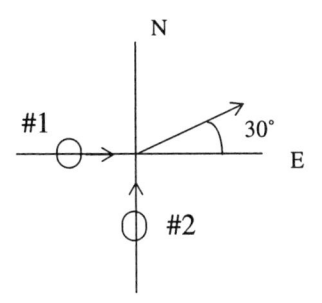

[Diagram: #1 moving east toward origin; #2 moving north toward origin; resultant at 30° north of east]

This is an inelastic collision. Only momentum is conserved.

For momentum along x-axis:

$$m_1 v_1 = (m_1 + m_2) v_f \cos\theta \qquad (1)$$

For momentum along y-axis:

$$m_2 v_2 = (m_1 + m_2) v_f \sin\theta \qquad (2)$$

$$\frac{m_2 v_2}{m_1 v_1} = \frac{(m_1 + m_2) v_f \sin\theta}{(m_1 + m_2) v_f \cos\theta}$$

$$\frac{m_2 v_2}{m_1 v_1} = \tan\theta$$

$$v_2 = \frac{m_1 v_1}{m_2} \tan\theta = \frac{80 \times 8}{75} \tan 30° = 4.9$$

$$v_2 = 4.9 \text{ m/s}$$

Using equation (2),

$$v_f = \frac{m_2 v_2}{(m_1 + m_2) \sin\theta} = \frac{75 \times 4.9}{(80 + 75) \sin 30°} = 4.8$$

$$v_f = 4.8 \text{ m/s}$$

(Inelastic collision)

19.

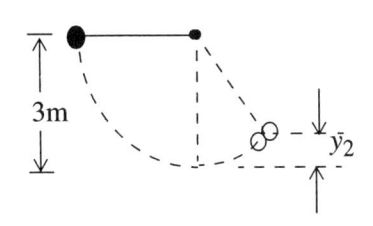

[Diagram: ball drops from height 3m, swings down and collides, with y_2 indicated]

From conservation of energy,

$$m_1 g y_1 = \frac{1}{2} m_1 v_1^2$$

$$v_1^2 = 2gy_1$$

From conservation of momentum,

$$m_1v_1 = (m_1 + m_2)v_2$$

$$v_2 = \frac{m_1v_1}{(m_1 + m_2)}$$

From conservation of energy,

$$\frac{1}{2}(m_1 + m_2)v_2^2 = (m_1 + m_2)gy_2$$

$$y_2 = \frac{v_2^2}{2g} = \left(\frac{m_1v_1}{m_1 + m_2}\right)^2/(2g)$$

$$y_2 = \left(\frac{m_1}{m_1 + m_2}\right)^2 y_1$$

$$y_2 = \left(\frac{85}{85 + 55}\right)^2 \times 3$$

$$y_2 = 1.11 \text{ m}$$

(Inelastic collision)

20.

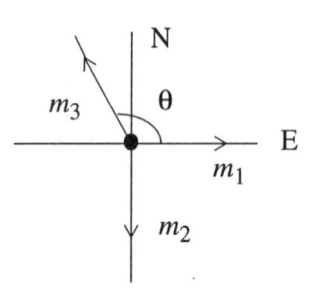

For momentum along x-axis,

$$0 = m_1v_1 + m_3v_3\cos\theta$$

$$m_3v_3\cos\theta = -m_1v_1 \quad (1)$$

For momentum along y-axis,

$$0 = -m_2v_2 + m_3v_3\sin\theta$$

$$m_3v_3\sin\theta = m_2v_2 \quad (2)$$

So, $\dfrac{m_3v_3\sin\theta}{m_3v_3\cos\theta} = \dfrac{m_2v_2}{-m_1v_1}$

$$\tan\theta = \frac{m_2 v_2}{-m_1 v_1} = -\frac{5.5 \times 2}{2 \times 4} = -1.375$$

$$\theta = -54°$$

In the second quadrant, $\theta = 126°$

From equation (1),

$$m_3 v_3 \cos\theta = -m_1 v_1$$

$$(3.5)v_3(\cos 126°) = -(2)(4)$$

$$-2.06 v_3 = -8$$

$$v_3 = 3.9 \text{ m/s}$$

(Inelastic collision)

21.

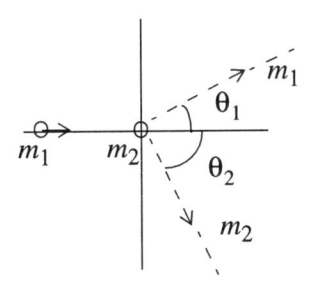

This being an elastic collision, KE must be conserved.

$$\frac{1}{2}mv_{1i}^2 = \frac{1}{2}mv_{1f}^2 + \frac{1}{2}mv_{2f}^2 \quad \text{(Note } m_1 = m_2\text{)}$$

$$v_{1i}^2 = v_{1f}^2 + v_{2f}^2 \tag{1}$$

$$6.5^2 = 3.5^2 + v_{2f}^2$$

$$v_{2f} = \sqrt{6.5^2 - 3.5^2} = 5.47$$

$$v_{2f} = 5.47 \text{ m/s}$$

Equation (1) above clearly shows that v_{1i}, v_{1f} and v_{2f} form a right triangle. The hypotenuse is v_{1i}.

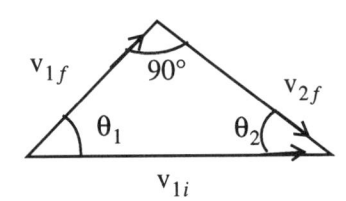

So, $\tan\theta_2 = \dfrac{v_{1f}}{v_{2f}} = \dfrac{3.5}{5.47} = 0.64$

$\theta_2 = 32.6°$

The second puck moves at 5.47 m/s in a direction 32.6° south of east.

(Elastic collision)

22. (a) Force of friction, $f = \mu N = \mu mg$

For opposing frictional force,

$-ma = \mu mg$

$a = -\mu g = -0.3 \times 9.8 = -2.94$ (1)

$v^2 = v_o^2 + 2ax$

$v^2 = 12^2 + 2(-2.94)1.5$

$v^2 = 144 - 8.82$

$v = 11.6$

So, just before collision

$v_{1i} = 11.6$ m/s

From conservation of momentum just after collision,

$m_1 v_{1i} = m_1 v_{1f} + m_2 v_{2f}$

$(10)(11.6) = 10 v_{1f} + 20 v_{2f}$

$v_{1f} = 11.6 - 2 v_{2f}$ (2)

From conservation of kinetic energy,

$\frac{1}{2} m_1 v_{1i}^2 = \frac{1}{2} m_1 v_{1f}^2 + \frac{1}{2} m_2 v_{2f}^2$

$(10)(11.6)^2 = (10) v_{1f}^2 + (20) v_{2f}^2$

$134.6 = v_{1f}^2 + 2 v_{2f}^2$

Using equation (2),

$134.6 = (11.6 - 2 v_{2f})^2 + 2 v_{2f}^2$

$134.6 = 134.6 - 46.4 v_{2f} + 4 v_{2f}^2 + 2 v_{2f}^2$

$0 = 6 v_{2f}^2 - 46.4 v_{2f} = v_{2f}(6 v_{2f} - 46.4)$

$v_{2f} = 0$ or,

$6v_{2f} - 46.4 = 0$

That is, $v_{2f} = 7.7$ m/s

$v_{2f} = 0$ is unacceptable for conservation of momentum.

So, $v_{2f} = 7.7$ m/s

From equation (2), $v_{1f} = 11.6 - 2 \times 7.7 = -3.8$

$$v_{1f} = -3.8 \text{ m/s}$$

(b) $v_2^2 = v_{2i}^2 + 2ax_2$

$0 = 7.7^2 + 2(-2.94)x_2$

$x_2 = 10.1$

$v_1^2 = v_{1i}^2 + 2ax_1$

$0 = (-3.8)^2 + 2(-2.94)x_1$

$x_1 = 2.46$

(Elastic collision)

23. The center of mass of the shell travels like an ordinary projectile.

$v_{ox} = v_o \cos\theta_o = (250)\cos 40° = 191.5$ m/s

$v_{oy} = v_o \sin\theta_o = (250)\sin 40° = 160.7$ m/s

Time of flight is obtained from,

$v = v_o + at$

$-v_{oy} = v_{oy} + at$

$at = -2v_{oy}$

$t = \dfrac{-2v_{oy}}{a} = \dfrac{2 \times 160.7}{-(-9.8)} = 32.8$ s

$x = v_{ox}t = 191.5 \times 32.8 = 6280$

$x = 6280$ m

(Inelastic collision)

Grade Yourself

Circle the question numbers that you had incorrect. Then indicate the number of questions you missed. If you answered more than three questions incorrectly, you need to focus on that topic. (If a topic has less than three questions and you had at least one wrong, we suggest you study that topic also. Read your textbook, a review book, or ask your teacher for help.)

Subject: Momentum and Impulse

Topic	Question Numbers	Number Incorrect
Impulse/momentum	1, 2, 5, 6, 10, 11, 13	
Elastic collision	4, 8, 12, 17, 21, 22	
Inelastic collision	3, 7, 9, 14, 15, 16, 18, 19, 20, 23	

Rotational Motion

Brief Yourself

There are two kinds of physical motion of an object. These are translational motion and rotational motion. Rotational or angular motion always takes place about an axis. Physical quantities describing angular motion are angular velocity and angular acceleration, which are closely related to the analogous quantities of translational motion.

Angular velocity and angular acceleration:

Angular velocity is defined as:

$$\omega = \Delta\theta/\Delta t \tag{1}$$

where the angular displacement $\Delta\theta = \theta - \theta_0$

and the time interval $\Delta t = t - t_0$.

Angular acceleration:

$$\alpha = \Delta\omega/\Delta t \tag{2}$$

where the change in angular velocity $\Delta\omega = \omega - \omega_0$.

Linear quantities are related to angular quantities by simple relations.

Arc length $s = r\theta$

where r is the radius of curvature and θ is the angle subtended by the arc of length s.

Linear velocity $v = \omega r$ and

linear acceleration $a = \alpha r$.

Equations describing angular motion are similar to the analogous equations of translational motion.

$$\omega = \omega_0 + \alpha t \tag{3}$$

$$\theta = \omega_0 t + (1/2)\alpha t^2 \tag{4}$$

$$\omega^2 = \omega_0^2 + 2\alpha\theta \tag{5}$$

Circular motion

One of the most familiar types of angular motion is Uniform Circular motion. Whenever an object undergoes a uniform circular motion, its acceleration is directed toward the center of the circle and is called centripetal acceleration. Its magnitude is constant and is given by

$$a_c = v^2/r \tag{6}$$

Using the relation for v above, the centripetal acceleration can also be written as:

$$a_c = \omega^2 r$$

When a force is a direct result of such acceleration, it is called centripetal force. We may write centripetal force as:

$$F_c = ma_c = mv^2/r = m\omega^2 r \tag{7}$$

Example of centripetal acceleration is the circular motion of the moon or a satellite about the earth. The centripetal acceleration on the moon due to earth's gravity is:

$$a_c = GM/r^2 \tag{8}$$

G = universal gravitational constant

M = mass of the Earth

r = distance between the Moon and the Earth

The centripetal force on the Moon due to Earth's gravity is:

$$F = G(Mm/r^2) \tag{9}$$

where m = mass of the moon.

In every rotational motion, a quantity analogous to mass comes into play. It is called the moment of inertia. Whenever the mass of an object can be treated as a point mass, the moment of inertia of such an object is:

$$I = mr^2 \tag{10}$$

where r is the distance of the object of mass m from the axis of rotation. More complex bodies have different formulas for calculating their moments of inertia. When an object undergoes angular motion, its kinetic energy of rotation is:

$$KE = (1/2)I\omega^2 \tag{11}$$

The angular momentum L of a body is defined as:

$$L = I\omega \tag{12}$$

Conservation of angular momentum for an isolated system of objects requires that

Total Initial Angular Momentum = Total Final Angular Momentum

A force is required to produce or to change the state of translational motion of a body. Similarly, a quantity called torque is required to produce or to change the state of rotational motion of a body.

The analog of force in rotational motion is called Torque. Torque τ about an axis can be defined as:

$$\tau = I\alpha \qquad (13)$$

where I is called moment of inertia.

When work is done by applying a torque on a body, work done is defined as:

$$W = \tau\theta \qquad (14)$$

where θ is the angle of rotation or angular displacement.

Test Yourself

1. The bob of a simple pendulum of length 0.75 m swings freely from rest through an arc length of 15 cm. Find the total angle it swings in degrees.

2. Starting from rest, a wheel rotates with a constant acceleration and achieves a final angular velocity of 10 rad/s in 5s. Find the
   (a) angular acceleration of the wheel
   (b) angle in radians through which it rotates during this time.

3. A horizontal spinning wheel rotates at 45 rad/s about its symmetric axis. It is brought to a stop in 20 seconds by applying a brake. Find the angular acceleration of the wheel.

4. The Earth spins on its own axis while it rotates about the sun. Find the
   (a) Earth's angular velocity about its own axis.
   (b) angular velocity of the earth about the sun.

5. Electron in the hydrogen atom moves at a constant speed of 2.2×10^6 m/s in a circle around the nucleus of the atom. The centripetal acceleration of the electron is 9.13×10^{22} m/s². Find the
   (a) radius of the electron orbit.
   (b) number of revolutions per second made by the electron.

6. An electric motor of a grinding wheel initially rotating at 100 rev/s is turned off. Assuming a constant angular deceleration of 1.5 rad/s², how long will it take for the motor to come to a halt?

7. A wheel initially at rest, is rotated with a constant acceleration of 4 rad/s² for 15s. The wheel is then brought to rest in 25 revolutions by applying a constant deceleration. Find the deceleration and the time it takes to bring the wheel to a stop from its maximum speed.

8. A toy car completes one cycle of uniform circular motion in 40 seconds around a horizontal circular track of radius 1.5 m. What is the centripetal acceleration of the toy car?

9. The speed of the tip of the minute hand of a grandfather wall clock is 2.5×10^{-3} m/s. What is the speed of the tip of the second hand of the same length?

10. A front door of a car requires a torque of 50 N·m to swing it open. The handle of the door is 0.75 m away from the axis where the hinges are attached. What is the minimum force needed to open the door?

11. Janet (mass 95 kg) rides a bicycle with pedals that are placed 20 cm from the axle. What maximum torque can she apply using her body weight alone?

12. A swimmer standing stiffly on the edge of a high diving board starts a spin upward at a rate of 1.5 rev/s. On the way down, the diver curls up into

the tuck position and spins 3.5 times each second. If the moment of inertia of the diver is 80 kg·m² in the upward lift, find the moment of inertia in the tuck position.

13. A light meter stick with a heavy mass at the lower end is vertically suspended from a pivot at the upper end. With what frequency will it oscillate if set into motion?

14. A satellite is in a circular orbit moving at 6.9×10^3 m/s. The radius of the Earth is 6.37×10^6 m. Find the altitude of the satellite from the surface of the Earth.

15. A person exerts 250 N of force on the edge of a roulette wheel (moment of inertia = $(1/2)mr^2$), initially at rest, for 2 s, giving it a rotation in the horizontal plane. The mass of the wheel is 20 kg and its radius is 0.6 m. Ignoring friction, find the maximum angular velocity that can be produced.

16. A person can apply a maximum force of 250 N on the handle of a wrench to turn a bolt. The bolts will turn if a torque of 45 N·m is applied. What is the minimum length of the wrench needed?

17. At what angle should a bobsled turn be banked if the sled is to safely move at 30 m/s around a radius of 50 m?

18. A hoop of mass 0.3 kg (moment of inertia, $I = mr^2$) and radius 0.05 m rolls without slipping down an inclined plane from a height of 0.5 m. Find the linear velocity of the hoop at the bottom of the incline.

19. A children's merry-go-round in a park consists of a 300 kg solid horizontal disk (moment of inertia, $I = 1/2mr^2$) of radius 8.5 m. It rotates at a speed of 0.25 rev/s while a person of mass 150 kg takes a ride at the edge of the disk. How fast will the disk be rotating if the person walks 4 m along the radius toward the center?

20. A merry-go-round made up of a horizontal wheel ($I = mr^2$) of mass 500 kg and radius 7 m rotates at a speed of 0.2 rev/s with no passengers on it. A man of mass 160 kg quickly jumps up and sits on the edge of the wheel. Find the new speed of the wheel.

21. A bucket of mass 3 kg is attached to one end of a massless rope wound around a solid cylindrical pulley ($I = 1/2mr^2$) of mass 6 kg and radius 0.25 m. The arrangement is used to draw water from a well as shown in the figure. The bucket starts at the top of the well and falls down for 3 s before hitting the water. How deep is the well from the rest position of the bucket?

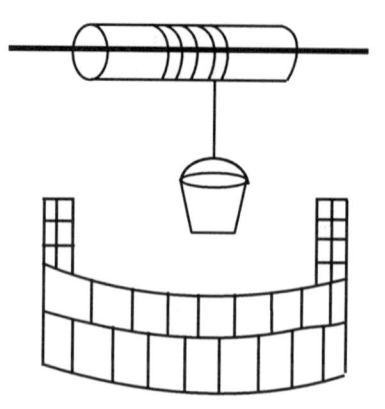

22. An ice-skater (moment of inertia = 2.0 kg·m²) with her hands stretched out spins at a speed of 5 rev/s. By closing her hands and legs inward she increases her speed by 500%. What is her new moment of inertia at the higher speed?

Check Yourself

1. Angle in radian = $\dfrac{\text{Arc length}}{\text{Radius}}$

$$\theta = \dfrac{0.15 \text{ m}}{0.75 \text{ m}}$$

$$\theta = 0.2 \text{ rad} = 11.4°$$

(Angular motion in general)

2. (a) $\omega = \omega_0 + \alpha t$

$$10 = 0 + \alpha(5)$$

$$\alpha = \dfrac{10}{5} = 2$$

$$\alpha = 2 \text{ rad/s}^2$$

(b) $\theta = \theta_0 + \omega_0 t + \dfrac{1}{2}\alpha t^2$

$$\theta = 0 + 0 + \dfrac{1}{2}(2)5^2$$

$$\theta = 25 \text{ rad}$$

(Angular motion in general)

3. $\omega = \omega_0 + \alpha t$

$$0 = 45 + \alpha(20)$$

$$\alpha = \dfrac{-45}{20}$$

$$\alpha = -2.25 \text{ rad/s}^2$$

(Angular motion in general)

4. (a) $\omega = \dfrac{\Delta \theta}{\Delta t} = \dfrac{2\pi \text{ rad}}{24 h} = \dfrac{2\pi}{24 \times 60 \times 60}$

$$\omega = 7.27 \times 10^{-5} \text{ rad/s}$$

(b) $\omega = \dfrac{2\pi}{365 \times 24 \times 3600} = 1.99\times10^{-7}$

$\omega = 1.99\times10^{-7}$ rad/s

(Uniform circular motion)

5. (a) $a_c = \dfrac{v^2}{r}$

$r = \dfrac{v^2}{a_c} = \dfrac{(2.2\times10^6)^2}{9.13\times10^{22}} = 5.3\times10^{-11}$

$r = 5.3\times10^{-11}$ m

(b) $f = \dfrac{\omega}{2\pi} = \dfrac{\omega r}{2\pi r} = \dfrac{v}{2\pi r} = \dfrac{2.2\times10^6}{2\pi \times 5.3\times10^{-11}}$

$f = 6.6\times10^{15}$ rev/s

(Angular motion in general)

6. $\omega = 100$ rev/s $= 100(2\pi)$ rad/s $= 200\pi$ rad/s

$\omega = \omega_0 + \alpha t$

$0 = 200\pi + (-1.5)t$

$t = \dfrac{200\pi}{1.5} = 4.19\times10^2$ s

$t = 6.98$ min

(Uniform circular motion)

7. In the first part of the problem,

$\omega = \omega_0 + \alpha t$

$\omega = 0 + 4(15)$

$\omega = 60$ rad/s^2

$\theta = 25$ rev. $= 25 \times 2\pi = 50\pi$ rad

$\omega^2 = \omega_0^2 - 2\alpha(\theta - \theta_0)$

$0 = 60^2 - 2\alpha(50\pi)$

$\alpha = \dfrac{60^2}{2 \times 50\pi}$

$\alpha = 11.5 \text{ rad/s}^2$

$\omega = \omega_0 - \alpha t$

$0 = 60 - (11.5)t$

$t = 5.22 \text{ s}$

(Angular motion in general)

8. $a_c = \dfrac{v^2}{r} = \dfrac{(\omega r)^2}{r} = \omega^2 r$

$\omega = \dfrac{2\pi}{40} = \dfrac{\pi}{20} \text{ rad/s}$

$a_c = \left(\dfrac{\pi}{20}\right)^2 1.5 = 3.70 \times 10^{-2}$

$a_c = 3.70 \times 10^{-2} \text{ m/s}^2$

(Uniform circular motion)

9. $v = \omega r = 2\pi f r = \dfrac{2\pi r}{T}$

$r = \dfrac{vT}{2\pi} = \dfrac{2.5 \times 10^{-3} \times 60 \times 60}{2\pi}$

$r = 1.43 \text{ m}$

The second hand has a time period, $T = 60 \text{ s}$

$v = \dfrac{2\pi r}{T} = \dfrac{2\pi \times 1.43}{60} = 0.15$

$v = 0.15 \text{ m/s}$ speed of second hand.

(Angular motion in general)

10. $\tau = 50 \text{ N} \cdot \text{m}$

$r = 0.75 \text{ m}$

$\tau = r \times F$

$\tau = rF \sin\theta$

$F = \dfrac{\tau}{r \sin\theta}, \theta = \dfrac{\pi}{2}$ for minimum force

$F = \dfrac{\tau}{r} = \dfrac{50}{0.75} = 66.7$

$F = 66.7$ N

(Torque)

11. $\tau = rF\sin\theta$

    $\tau = rMg\sin\theta$, $\theta = \dfrac{\pi}{2}$ for maximum torque.

    $\tau = 0.2 \times 95 \times 9.81 \times \sin\dfrac{\pi}{2} = 1.86 \times 10^2$

    $\tau = 1.86 \times 10^2$ N · m

(Torque)

12. Angular momentum must be conserved.

    $I_1\omega_1 = I_2\omega_2$

    $I_1 = 80$ (kg · m^2), $\omega_1 = 1.5$ rev/s, $\omega_2 = 3.5$ rev/s

    $I_2 = \dfrac{I_1\omega_1}{\omega_2} = \dfrac{80 \times 1.5}{3.5} = 34.3$

    $I_2 = 34.3$ (kg · m^2)

(Angular momentum)

13. $T = 2\pi\sqrt{\dfrac{l}{g}}$

    $f = \dfrac{1}{2\pi}\sqrt{\dfrac{g}{l}} = \dfrac{1}{2\pi}[9.81/1]^{\frac{1}{2}} = 0.498$

    $f = 0.5$ cycle/sec.

(Angular motion in general)

14. Gravitational force = Centripetal force

    $G\dfrac{Mm}{(r+R)^2} = m\dfrac{v^2}{(r+R)}$

    $(r + R) = \dfrac{GM}{v^2} = \dfrac{6.67 \times 10^{-11} \times 5.98 \times 10^{24}}{(6.9 \times 10^3)^2} = 8.38 \times 10^6$

    Altitude, $r = 2010$ km

(Uniform circular motion)

15. $\tau = rF = 0.6 \times 250 = 150$ N·m

$\tau = I\alpha = \left(\frac{1}{2}mr^2\right)\alpha = \frac{1}{2} \times 20 \times 0.6^2 \alpha = 3.6\alpha$

$3.6\alpha = 150$

$\alpha = \frac{150}{3.6}$

$\alpha = 41.7$ rad/s^2

$\omega = \omega_0 + \alpha t$

$= 0 + 41.7 \times 2$

$\omega = 83.4$ rad/s

(Torque)

16. Torque,

$\tau = rF\sin\theta$

$r = \frac{\tau}{F\sin\theta}, \theta = \frac{\pi}{2}$ for minimum r.

$r = \frac{45}{250} = 0.18$

$r = 18$ cm

(Torque)

17.

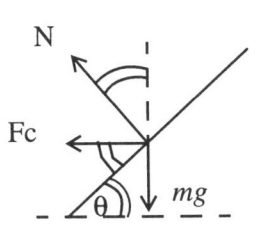

Centripetal force, $F_c = \frac{mv^2}{r}$

$\Sigma F_x = m\frac{v^2}{r}$ and $\Sigma F_y = 0$

For forces along x-axis,

$N\sin\theta = \frac{mv^2}{r}$ \hfill (1)

For forces along y-axis,

$N\cos\theta - mg = 0$

$\quad N\cos\theta = mg \hfill (2)$

Dividing the terms in equation (1) and (2),

$$\frac{N\sin\theta}{N\cos\theta} = \frac{mv^2/r}{mg}$$

$$\tan\theta = \frac{v^2}{gr}$$

$$= \frac{30^2}{9.81 \times 50}$$

$$\tan\theta = 1.835$$

$$\theta = 61.4°$$

(Uniform circular motion)

18. From conservation of energy

$$E_o = E_f$$

$$mgh = \frac{1}{2}mv^2 + \frac{1}{2}I\omega^2$$

$$= \frac{1}{2}mv^2 + \frac{1}{2}mr^2\omega^2$$

$$= \frac{1}{2}mv^2 + \frac{1}{2}mv^2$$

$$= mv^2$$

$$v^2 = gh = 9.8 \times 0.5 = 4.9$$

$$v = 2.2 \text{ m/s}$$

(Angular motion in general)

19. Angular momentum must be conserved.

$$I_1\omega_1 = I_2\omega_2$$

$$\omega_2 = \frac{I_1\omega_1}{I_2} \hfill (1)$$

$$I_1 = \frac{1}{2}MR^2 + mR^2 = \left(\frac{M}{2} + m\right)R^2$$

$$= \left(\frac{300}{2} + 150\right)8.5^2$$

$$= 300 \times 8.5^2 = 2.17 \times 10^4$$

$$I_1 = 2.17 \times 10^4 \text{ kg} \cdot \text{m}^2 \tag{2}$$

$$I_2 = \frac{1}{2}MR^2 + mr^2 = \frac{1}{2}(300)8.5^2 + 150(4.5)^2$$

$$I_2 = 1.39 \times 10^4 \text{ (kg} \cdot \text{m}^2) \tag{3}$$

$$\omega_2 = \frac{2.17 \times 10^4}{1.39 \times 10^4} \times (0.25)$$

$$\omega_2 = 0.39 \text{ rev/s}$$

(Angular momentum)

20. Angular momentum must be conserved.

$$I_1\omega_1 = I_2\omega_2$$

$$\omega_2 = \frac{I_1\omega_1}{I_2}$$

$$I_1 = MR^2 = 500 \times 7^2 = 2.45 \times 10^4 \text{ kg} \cdot \text{m}^2$$

$$I_2 = MR^2 + mR^2 = (M+m)R^2$$

$$= (500 + 150)7^2 = 3.185 \times 10^4 \text{ kg} \cdot \text{m}^2$$

$$\omega_2 = \frac{I_1\omega_1}{I_2} = \frac{2.45 \times 10^4 \times 0.2}{3.185 \times 10^4}$$

$$\omega_2 = 0.15 \text{ rev/s}$$

(Angular momentum)

21. Energy must be conserved.

Initial PE of bucket = KE of bucket after fall + Rotational KE of pulley

$$Mgh = \frac{1}{2}Mv^2 + \frac{1}{2}I\omega^2$$

$$= \frac{1}{2}Mv^2 + \left(\frac{1}{2}\right)\frac{1}{2}(mr^2)\omega^2$$

$$Mgh = \frac{1}{2}Mv^2 + \frac{1}{4}mv^2$$

$$Mgh = v^2\left(\frac{1}{2}M + \frac{1}{4}m\right)$$

$$v^2 = \left(\frac{Mgh}{\frac{M}{2}+\frac{m}{4}}\right) = \left(\frac{3\times 9.81}{1.5+1.5}\right)h = 9.81h \tag{1}$$

Also, $v^2 = v_0^2 + 2a(y-y_0)$

$$v^2 = 2ah \tag{2}$$

Therefore, $2ah = 9.81h$

Therefore, $a = \dfrac{9.81}{2} = 4.905$

$$y = y_0 + v_{oy}t + \frac{1}{2}at^2$$

$$(y - y_0) = \frac{1}{2}at^2$$

$$h = \frac{1}{2}(4.905)3^2 = 22.1$$

$h = 22.1$ m

(Angular motion in general)

22.   Angular momentum is conserved.

$I_1\omega_1 = I_2\omega_2$

$I_2 = \dfrac{I_1\omega_1}{\omega_2}$, $\omega_2 = 5\omega_1$

$I_2 = \dfrac{2.0\times 5}{5\times 5}$

$I_2 = 0.4$ kg·m^2

(Angular momentum)

Grade Yourself

Circle the question numbers that you had incorrect. Then indicate the number of questions you missed. If you answered more than three questions incorrectly, you need to focus on that topic. (If a topic has less than three questions and you had at least one wrong, we suggest you study that topic also. Read your textbook, a review book, or ask your teacher for help.)

Subject: Rotational Motion

Topic	Question Numbers	Number Incorrect
Angular motion in general	1, 2, 3, 5, 7, 9, 13, 18, 21	
Uniform circular motion	4, 6, 8, 14, 17	
Angular momentum	12, 19, 20, 22	
Torque	10, 11, 15, 16	

Objects in Equilibrium

9

Brief Yourself

The motion of an object is produced by forces and torques acting on it. If the forces acting on a body completely cancel each other out, the body is in translational equilibrium. This means the body may be completely at rest or moving at uniform velocity. Under this situation, force being a vector, the sum of the forces along each axis is zero. Mathematically, we may write:

$$\sum F_x = 0$$

$$\sum F_y = 0$$

$$\sum F_z = 0.$$

For example, if three forces acting on a body produce no acceleration, then

$$F_{1x} + F_{2x} + F_{3x} = 0$$

$$F_{1y} + F_{2y} + F_{3y} = 0$$

$$F_{1z} + F_{2z} + F_{3z} = 0$$

Similarly, when the sum of the torques applied on a body is zero, the body is in rotational equilibrium. This means either the complete absence of rotation or the presence of rotation at uniform angular velocity. Under this situation, the sum of the torques about any chosen axis acting on the body will be zero. We may express it mathematically as follows:

$$\sum \tau_i = 0$$

For example, if three torques acting on a body produce no angular acceleration, then these torques about any axis will be zero. That is:

$$\tau_1 + \tau_2 + \tau_3 = 0$$

Test Yourself

1. A simple pendulum consists of a string and a ball of mass 5 kg. It is vertically suspended from the ceiling of a room. Find the tension in the string when the ball is at rest.

2. A block of mass 15 kg is placed on an inclined plane making an angle of 35° with the horizontal. Find the minimum coefficient of friction between the block and the plane necessary to prevent the block from sliding down.

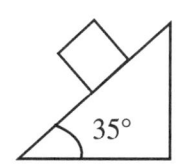

3. In a playground, a 20 kg girl sits on a seesaw 2.5 m from the fulcrum. How close to the fulcrum should her 115 kg mother sit to counter the girl's weight? (Ignore the mass of the seesaw.)

4. A construction worker can apply a force of 950 N on one end of a crowbar that is 1.5 m long. How large a force can be supported if the fulcrum is placed at 0.25 m from the other end?

5. A meter stick of mass 0.25 kg is horizontally balanced on a knife edge with two masses placed on it. One mass of 0.55 kg is placed at the 15 cm mark and the other of 0.75 kg is placed at the 90 cm mark. Find the force and position of the knife edge.

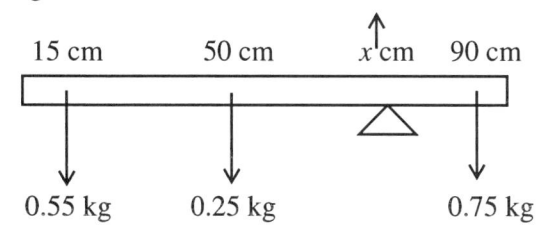

6. A 125 kg sign painter stands in equilibrium on a uniform horizontal board of mass 250 kg and length 15m as shown in the figure. Find the tensions in the vertical cables at the two ends of the board if the painter stands 4 m from the right end.

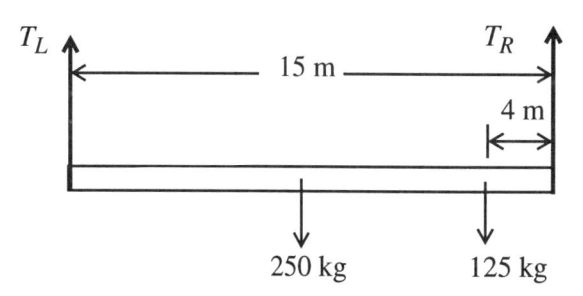

7. A 90 kg diver stands at the edge of a 5 m diving board. The diving board is supported by two pedestals 0.75 m apart as shown. The mass of the diving board is negligible. Calculate the two forces exerted by the two pedestals.

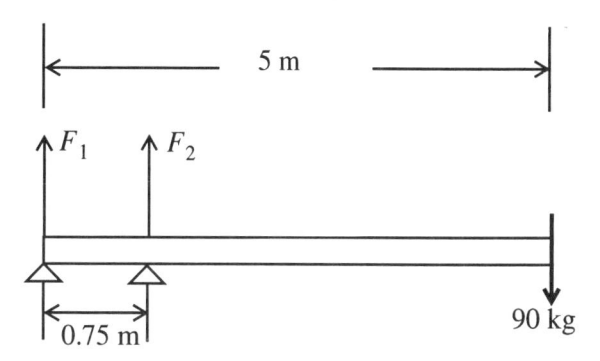

8. A car is stuck on the side of a road in a snow storm. The driver attaches one end of a 10 m rope to the car and uses a nearby tree to tie the other end of the rope, allowing just a little slack as shown. The rope is inextensible. The driver can exert a force of 600 N on the rope in the middle. What will be the maximum force on the car?

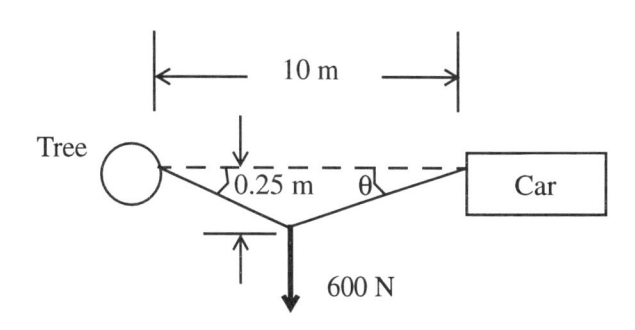

9. A traffic light of mass 30 kg at a road intersection is vertically suspended by three cables. Two of the cables make angles of 30° and 60° with the

horizontal as shown in the figure below. Find the three tensions in the three cables.

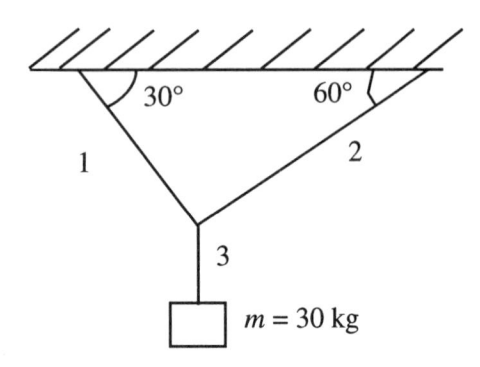

30° 60°
1   2
   3
   m = 30 kg

10. A commando weighing 1,000 N starts monkey crawling on a stout horizontal rope that is tied to two trees (100 m apart) on the two banks of a river as shown. Unfortunately, the rope breaks when the commando reaches the middle of the rope. Find the tension on the rope that resulted in this misfortune.

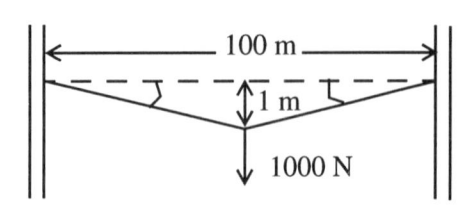

100 m
1 m
1000 N

11. Two boatmen pull on two ropes from two banks of a narrow channel to tug a boat at a constant speed as shown. Each exerts 750 N directed at 25° to the forward motion of the boat. Find the opposing force exerted by the water on the boat.

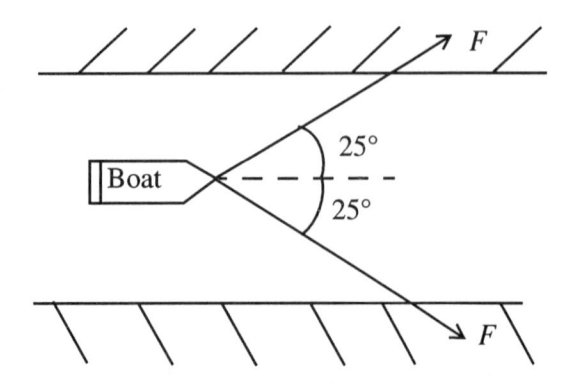

12. A block of mass $m_1 = 5$ kg placed on a horizontal rough table is tied to one end of a string that runs over a smooth pulley held at the edge of the table. A second block of mass $m_2 = 3$ kg that is tied to the other end of the string and suspended vertically as shown. What minimum coefficient of friction between the table top and mass m_1 must exist for the system to be at rest?

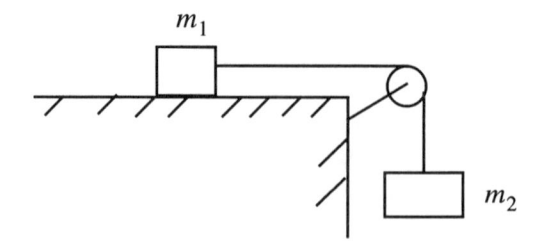

13. A 100 kg person safely climbs three fourths of the way from the bottom of a ladder leaning against a frictionless wall. The ladder is 12 m long and weighs 300 N. It makes an angle of 60° with the rough horizontal ground. Find the magnitude and direction of the force at the bottom of the ladder.

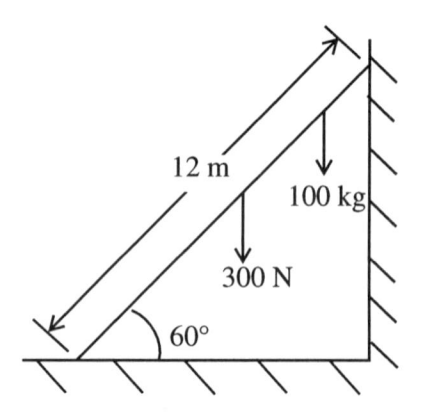

14. A rectangular door of length 1.5 m and width 0.75 m, is vertically held at rest by two hinges at one side of the door. The door has a uniformly distributed mass of 60 kg. Each hinge is 0.25 m from the nearest corner of the door and balances an equal amount of the force exerted by the weight of the door. Find the force exerted by each of the hinges on the door.

15. A 6 m long uniform and horizontal board of mass 80 kg rests on two supports each 1.5 m away from an end. A carpenter of mass 120 kg walks on the board toward the end. How close to the end can he walk without upsetting the balance?

16. A 50 kg ladder is 8 m long. It leans against a frictionless vertical wall and makes an angle of 50° with the rough horizontal ground. Find the force of friction between the ground and the ladder at the base.

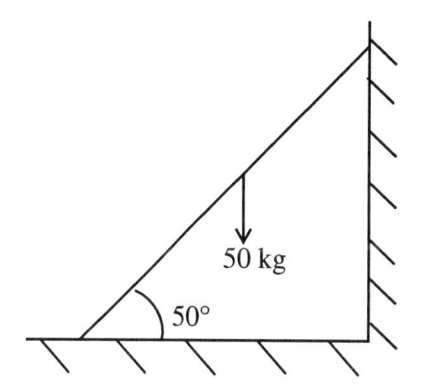

Check Yourself

1.

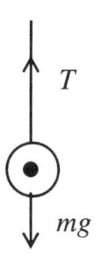

The force of gravity on the ball balances the tension upward in the string

$\Sigma F_y = 0$

$T - mg = 0$

$T = mg = 5 \times 9.81 = 49.0$ N upward

(Forces in equilibrium)

2.

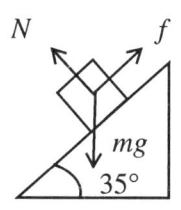

There are three forces acting on the block. These are the force of gravity downward, a normal restoring force exerted by the inclined plane, and the force of friction up the plane. We resolve these forces along the plane and perpendicular to the plane.

For the forces along the inclined plane, we have

$mg \sin 35° - f = 0$

$$mg\sin 35° - \mu N = 0 \qquad (1)$$

For the forces perpendicular to the inclined plane, we have

$$N - mg\cos 35° = 0$$

$$N = mg\cos 35° \qquad (2)$$

Using the value of N for equation (2) in equation (1) we obtain

$$mg\sin 35° - \mu mg\cos 35° = 0$$

$$mg\sin 35° = \mu mg\cos 35°$$

$$\mu \cos 35° = \sin 35°$$

$$\mu = \tan 35°$$

$$\mu = 0.7$$

(Forces in equilibrium)

3.

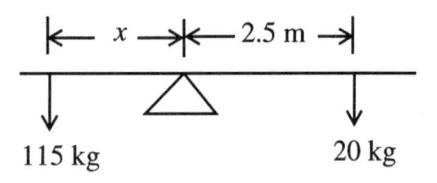

```
|← x →|← 2.5 m →|
    △
↓           ↓
115 kg      20 kg
```

Here the forces exerted and the torques produced must be balanced.

Force of gravity for child = $20 \times 9.81 = 196.2$ N

Force of gravity for mother = $115 \times 9.81 = 1128.1$ N

For balancing the torques about the axis at the fulcrum we have,

$$(1128.1) \times x - (196.2)2.5 = 0$$

$$1128.1x = 490.5$$

$$x = 0.43 \text{ m}$$

(Torques in equilibrium)

4.

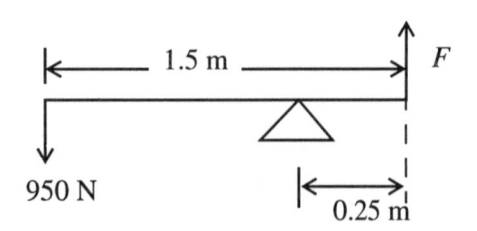

```
|←    1.5 m    →| F↑
       △
↓              |← →|
950 N           0.25 m
```

Here torques must be balanced.

$$950(1.5 - 0.25) - F(0.25) = 0$$

$$950(1.25) = 0.25F$$

$$F = 4750 \text{ N}$$

(Torques in equilibrium)

5.

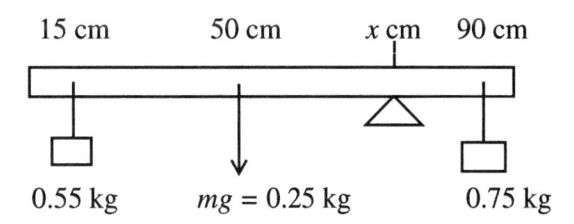

```
   15 cm      50 cm     x cm   90 cm
   ┌─────────────────────────────────┐
   │                        △        │
   └─────────────────────────────────┘
     │          ↓                │
   0.55 kg   mg = 0.25 kg     0.75 kg
```

Sum of the forces must be zero.

$$F - 0.55 \times 9.81 - 0.25 \times 9.81 - 0.75 \times 9.81 = 0$$

$$F = (0.55 + 0.25 + 0.75)9.81$$

$$F = 15.2 \text{ N}$$

Sum of torques must be zero.

$$(x-15)0.55 + (x-50)0.25 - (90-x)0.75 = 0$$

$$x(0.55 + 0.25 + 0.75) = 15 \times 0.55 + 50 \times 0.25 + 90 \times 0.75$$

$$1.55x = 88.25$$

$$x = 56.9 \text{ cm}$$

(Forces and torques in equilibrium)

6.

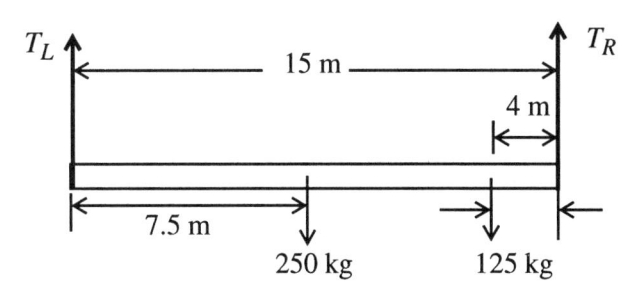

```
   T_L ↑                              ↑ T_R
       ←────── 15 m ──────→
                              ← 4 m →
   ┌───────────────────────────────────┐
   └───────────────────────────────────┘
       ← 7.5 m →
                ↓            ↓
              250 kg       125 kg
```

Forces and torques are balanced. We need to consider both for solving this problem.

For vertical forces we have,

$$T_L + T_R - 250 \times 9.81 - 125 \times 9.81 = 0$$

$$T_L + T_R = (250 + 125)9.81$$

$$T_R + T_L = 3.68 \times 10^3 \qquad (1)$$

For torques about an axis through the center of gravity of the board we have,

$$T_R(7.5) - T_L(7.5) - (125 \times 9.81)3.5 = 0$$

$$7.5(T_R - T_L) = 4.29 \times 10^3$$

$$T_R - T_L = 5.72 \times 10^2 \qquad (2)$$

Adding each side of equations (1) and (2) we get,

$$2T_R = 3.68 \times 10^3 + 5.72 \times 10^2 = 4.25 \times 10^3$$

$$T_R = 2.13 \times 10^3 \text{ N}$$

Subtracting each side of equation (2) from each side of equation (1) we get,

$$2T_L = 3.68 \times 10^3 - 5.72 \times 10^2 = 3.11 \times 10^3$$

$$T_L = 1.55 \times 10^3 \text{ N}$$

(Forces and torques in equilibrium)

7.

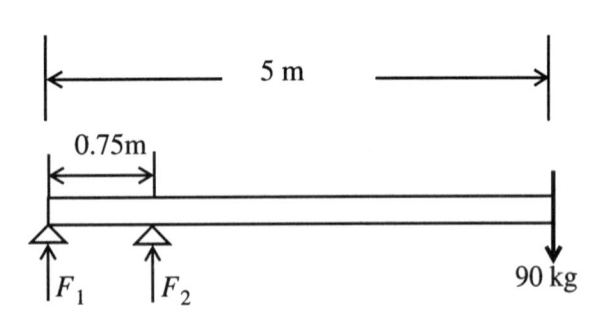

Considering the sum of the forces we have,

$$F_1 + F_2 - 90 \times 9.81 = 0$$

$$F_1 + F_2 = 90 \times 9.81 = 8.83 \times 10^2 \qquad (1)$$

Considering the torques about the axis at the edge of force F_1 we get,

$$F_2(0.75) - 90 \times 9.81 \times 5 = 0$$

$$0.75 F_2 = 4.41 \times 10^3$$

$$F_2 = 5.89 \times 10^3 \text{ N upward}$$

Using the value of F_2 in equation (1) we get,

$$F_1 + 5.89 \times 10^3 = 8.83 \times 10^2$$

$$F_1 = -5.00 \times 10^3 \text{ N downward}$$

(Forces and torques in equilibrium)

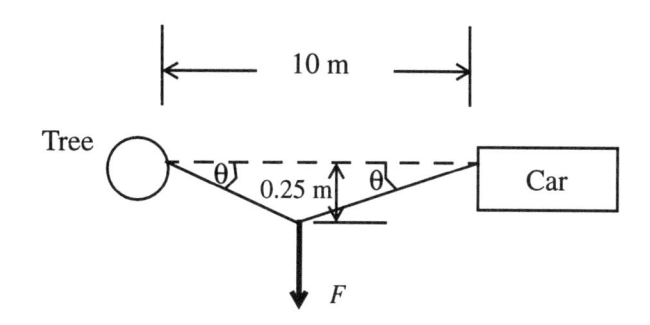

8.

$$\tan\theta = \frac{0.25}{5} = 0.05$$

$$\theta = 2.86°$$

$$\Sigma F_y = 0$$

$$T\sin\theta + T\sin\theta - F = 0$$

$$2T\sin\theta = F = 600$$

$$2T\sin 2.86° = 600$$

$$T = \frac{600}{2\sin 2.86°} = 6.01 \times 10^3 \text{ N}$$

Force on the car is 6.01×10^3 N.

(Forces in equilibrium)

9.

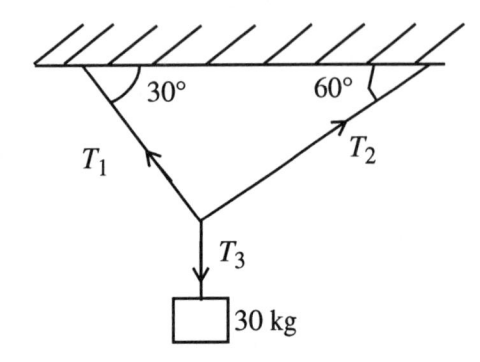

The free body force diagram of mass m is as follows:

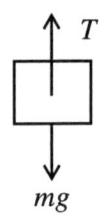

So, $\quad T - mg = 0$

$T = mg = 30 \times 9.81 = 294$

$T = 294 \text{ N}$

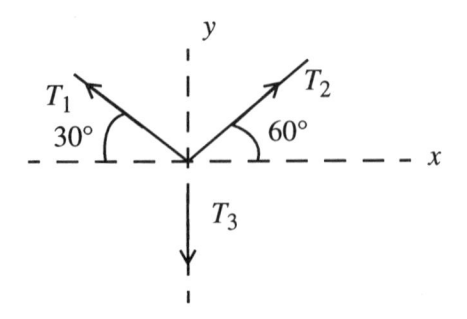

$\Sigma F_x = 0, T_2\cos 60° - T_1\cos 30° = 0$

$0.5T_2 - 0.866T_1 = 0$

$$T_2 = \frac{0.866}{0.5}T_1 = 1.732T_1 \qquad (1)$$

$\Sigma F_y = 0, T_1\sin 30° + T_2\sin 60° - T_3 = 0$

$0.5T_1 + (1.732T_1)0.866 - 294 = 0$

$0.5T_1 + 1.5T_1 = 294$

$2T_1 = 294$

$T_1 = 147 \text{ N}$

Using the value of T_1 in equation (1), we get $T_2 = 1.732 T_1 = 1.732 \times 147$

$T_2 = 255$ N

(Forces in equilibrium)

10.

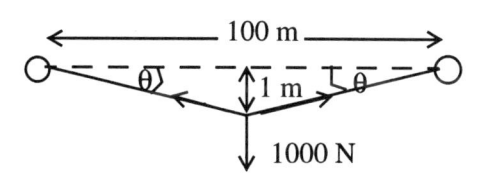

$$\tan\theta = \frac{1}{50} = 0.02$$

$$\theta = 1.15°$$

$$\Sigma F_y = 0$$

$$T\sin\theta + T\sin\theta = 1000$$

$$2T\sin\theta = 1000$$

$$T\sin 1.15° = 500$$

$$T = 2.49 \times 10^4 \text{ N}$$

(Forces in equilibrium)

11.

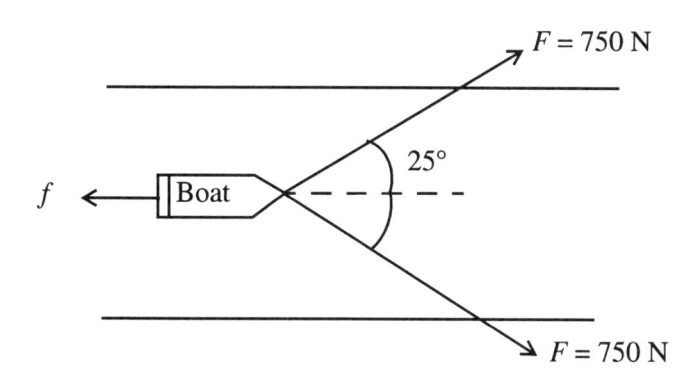

Let f be the force exerted by the water. For forces along x-axis

$$\Sigma F_x = 0$$

$$F\cos 25 + F\cos 25° - f = 0$$

$$2F\cos 25° = f$$

$$f = 2F\cos 25° = 2 \times 750 \times \cos 25°$$

$f = 1.36 \times 10^3$ N backward

(Forces in equilibrium)

12.

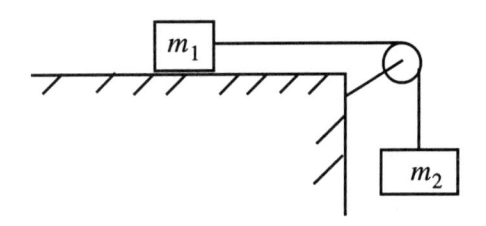

$W_1 = m_1 g = 5 \times 9.81 = 49.1$ N

$W_2 = m_2 g = 3 \times 9.81 = 29.4$ N

The free body force diagram for mass m_1 is

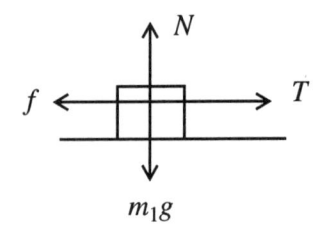

For forces along x-axis,

$\Sigma F = 0, T - f = 0, T = f$

For forces along y-axis,

$\Sigma F_y = 0, N - m_1 g = 0, N = m_1 g$

So, $T = f = \mu N = \mu m_1 g$ (1)

The free body diagram of forces for mass m_2 is

$\Sigma F_y = 0, T = m_2 g$ (2)

Using value of T in equation (1) we get

$m_2 g = \mu m_1 g$

Therefore, $\mu = \dfrac{m_2}{m_1} = \dfrac{3}{5}$

$\mu = 0.6$

(Forces in equilibrium)

13.

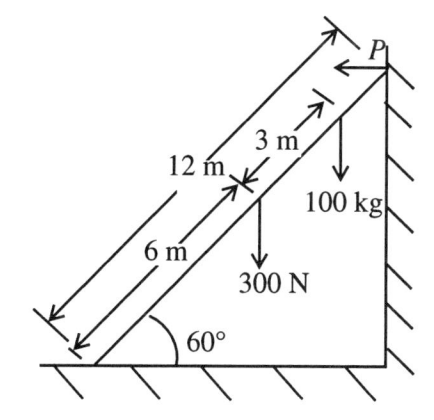

Sum of the torques on the ladder must be zero. So, torques about the axis at the bottom of the ladder,

$$P(12)\sin 60° - (300)(6)\cos 60° - (100)(9.81)(9)\cos 60° = 0$$

$$P(12)(0.866) - 900 - 4.41 \times 10^3 = 0$$

$$10.392P = 5.31 \times 10^3$$

$$P = 5.11 \times 10^2 \tag{1}$$

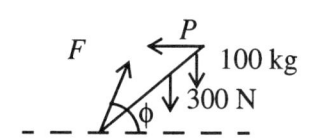

$$\Sigma F_x = 0$$

$$F\cos\phi - P = 0$$

$$F\cos\phi = P = 5.11 \times 10^2 \tag{2}$$

$$\Sigma F_y = 0$$

$$F\sin\phi - 300 - 100 \times 9.81 = 0$$

$$F\sin\phi - 300 - 981 = 0$$

$$F\sin\phi = 1281 \tag{3}$$

Squaring each side of equations (2) and (3) and adding we get,

$$(F\cos\phi)^2 + (F\sin\phi)^2 = (5.11\times10^2)^2 + (1281)^2$$

$$F^2(\cos^2\phi + \sin^2\phi) = 1.90\times10^6$$

$$F^2 = 1.90\times10^6$$

$$F = 1.38\times10^3 \text{ N}$$

Dividing each side of equation (3) by each side of equation (2) we get,

$$\frac{F\sin\phi}{F\cos\phi} = \frac{1281}{5.11\times10^2}$$

$$\tan\phi = 2.51$$

$$\phi = 68.2°$$

(Forces and torques in equilibrium)

14.

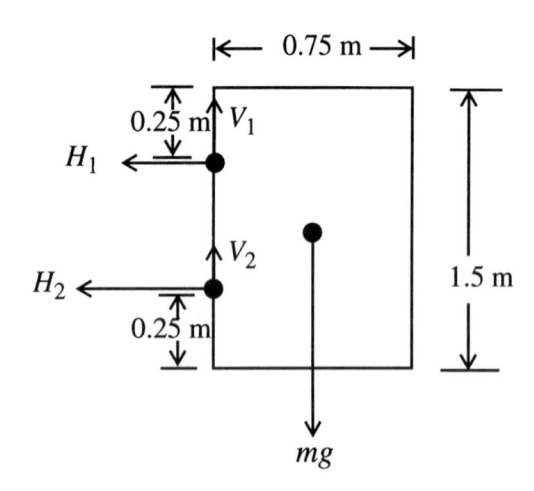

Here H and V are the symbols for horizontal and vertical forces at the hinge.

By condition of the problem, we define:

$$V_1 = V_2 = V$$

$$\Sigma F_y = 0,$$

$$V_1 + V_2 - mg = 0$$

$$2V - mg = 0$$

$$V = \frac{mg}{2} = \frac{60 \times 9.81}{2} = 2.94\times10^2$$

So, $V_1 = V_2 = 2.94\times10^2$ N

$$\Sigma F_x = 0$$

$H_1 + H_2 = 0$

$H_2 = -H_1$

So, define $|H_1| = |H_2| = H$

Torques about the axis passing through lower hinge,

$-(mg)(0.375) + H_1(1) = 0$

$H_1 = (0.375)60 \times 9.81 = 2.21 \times 10^2$

Therefore, $H_1 = 2.21 \times 10^2$ N

$H_2 = -2.21 \times 10^2$ N

Magnitude of force at each hinge is the same.

$F_{lower} = F_{upper} = \sqrt{H^2 + V^2} = \sqrt{[(2.21 \times 10^2)^2 + (2.94 \times 10^2)^2]}$

$F = (13.53 \times 10^4)^{\frac{1}{2}}$

$F = 3.68 \times 10^2$ N

$\tan\phi = \frac{V}{H} = \frac{2.94 \times 10^2}{2.21 \times 10^2} = 1.33$

$\phi = 53.1°$

So, the magnitude and direction of the force at the lower hinge are 3.68×10^2 N and $53.1°$, respectively.

And the magnitude and direction of the force at upper hinge are 3.68×10^2 N and $126.9°$ (2nd quadrant), respectively.

(Forces and torques in equilibrium)

15.

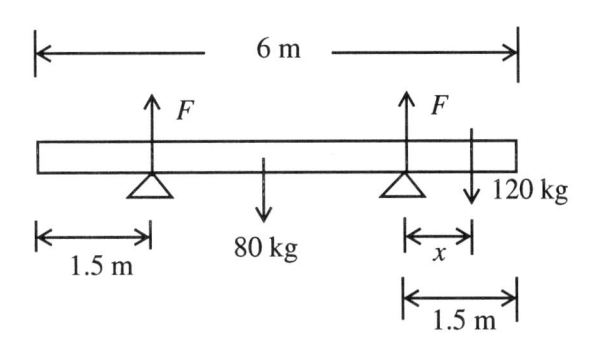

Let the carpenter stand at distance x from the right support before upsetting the balance.

At that point, the left support will be free of any force. Balancing the torques about an axis passing through the right support we have,

$$(80)(9.81)(1.5) - 120(9.81)x = 0$$

$$1.18 \times 10^3 - 1.18 \times 10^3 x = 0$$

$$x = 1 \text{ m}$$

(Torques in equilibrium)

16.

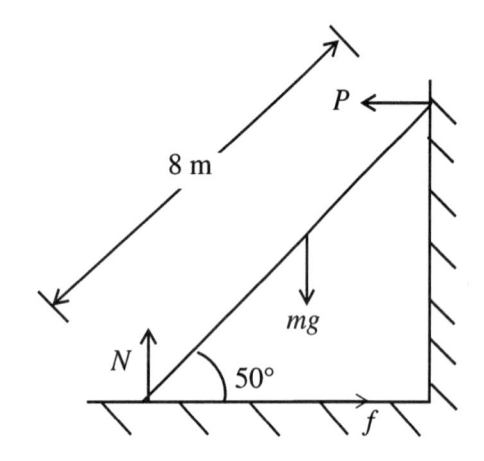

Force of friction = f

Normal force at the base = N

Weight of the ladder = $50 \times 9.81 = 4.9 \times 10^2$ N

Normal force of the wall = P

$$\Sigma F_x = 0$$

$$f - P = 0$$

$$P = f \tag{1}$$

$$\Sigma F_y = 0$$

$$N - mg = 0$$

$$N = mg = 4.9 \times 10^2 \tag{2}$$

Torques about an axis at the base of the ladder are,

$$-(mg)(4)\cos 50° + P(8)\sin 50° = 0$$

$$-50 \times 9.81 \times 4 \times \cos 50° + 6.128P = 0$$

$$P = \frac{1.26 \times 10^3}{6.128} = 2.06 \times 10^2 \tag{3}$$

Using the value of P in equation 1,

$f = 2.06 \times 10^2$ N

(Forces and torques in equilibrium)

Grade Yourself

Circle the question numbers that you had incorrect. Then indicate the number of questions you missed. If you answered more than three questions incorrectly, you need to focus on that topic. (If a topic has less than three questions and you had at least one wrong, we suggest you study that topic also. Read your textbook, a review book, or ask your teacher for help.)

Subject: Objects in Equilibrium

Topic	Question Numbers	Number Incorrect
Forces in equilibrium	1, 2, 8, 9, 10, 11, 12	
Torques in equilibrium	3, 4, 15	
Forces and torques in equilibrium	5, 6, 7, 13, 14, 16	

Fluid Mechanics

10

Brief Yourself

There are three states or phases of matter. These are solid, liquid, and gas. Liquids and gases are unable to keep their shape intact. They are collectively called fluids.

Density and Specific Gravity:

One measure of whether a substance is heavier or lighter is given by the term *density*. Density ρ is defined as:

$$\rho = \frac{\text{Mass}}{\text{Volume}} = \frac{m}{V} \tag{1}$$

There is one other way to express the heaviness or lightness of a substance. The term used is called *specific gravity* (sp gr). Specific gravity is the ratio of the density of the substance to the density of water at 4°C. We may write it as follows:

$$\text{sp gr} = \frac{\text{Density of substance}}{\text{Density of water}} \tag{2}$$

Archimedes Principle:

It states that the upward buoyant force exerted on an immersed object is equal to the weight of the volume of the fluid displaced by the object. It can be written as:

Force upward = Weight of the displaced fluid

Pressure:

In the study of fluid motion, pressure is an important measure of force applied. It is defined as:

$$\text{Pressure} = P = \frac{\text{Force}}{\text{Area on which the force is applied}}$$

In a streamline flow of liquid through a pipe, the flow rate of liquid is constant. It is given by the equation of continuity. It is expressed as follows:

Rate of flow = $A_1 v_1 = A_2 v_2$ = constant

where the velocity and area of cross section of the liquid at point #1 are v_1 and A_1, respectively, and at point #2, v_2 and A_2.

Pascal's Principle:

Pressure applied on any part of a confined fluid (liquid or gas) is equally shared by every part of the same confined fluid.

Pressure exerted by a column of fluid of height h and density ρ is:

$$P = \rho g h$$

where g is acceleration due to gravity.

Bernoulli's equation relating to the pressure at two different points in a stream line flow of liquid is:

$$P_1 + (\tfrac{1}{2})\rho (v_1)^2 + \rho g h_1 = P_2 + (\tfrac{1}{2})\rho (v_2)^2 + \rho g h_2 \tag{3}$$

Elastic Properties of Solids:

Forces acting on a body may temporarily or permanently deform the body. Elastic property of a body is related to its ability to regain the original shape of the body after the forces are removed. Forces acting on the body are measured in terms of stress.

$$\text{Stress} = \frac{\text{Force}}{\text{Surface area over which the force acts}} = \frac{F}{A}$$

The deformation of a body under stress is measured by a quantity called strain.

$$\text{Strain} = \frac{\text{Change in dimension}}{\text{Original dimension}}$$

Hooke's law states that the stress applied on a body is proportional to the strain suffered by the body, in particular:

$$\text{Modulus of Elasticity} = \frac{\text{Stress}}{\text{Strain}} \tag{4}$$

In the case of a body under longitudinal stress:

$$\text{Young's modulus} = Y = \frac{\text{Tensile stress}}{\text{Tensile strain}}$$

$$Y = [F/A]/[\Delta L/L_0] = \frac{F L_o}{A(\Delta L)} \tag{5}$$

In the case of stress produced by parallel forces on the surface of a body:

$$\text{Shear modulus} = S = \frac{\text{Shearing stress}}{\text{Shearing strain}}$$

$$S = [F/A]/[\Delta L/h] = \frac{F}{A(\tan \phi)} \tag{6}$$

where h is the height and ϕ is the shear angle in radians.

In the case of stress that results in the change of volume:

$$\text{Bulk modulus} = B = \frac{\text{Volume stress}}{\text{Volume strain}}$$

$$B = [F/A]/[\Delta V/V] \tag{7}$$

Ideal Spring and Simple Harmonic Motion:

We may rewrite the equation (5) in the following way:

$$F = \left[\frac{YA}{L_o}\right]\Delta L = [k]x \tag{8}$$

The quantity in the brackets can be treated as a constant equal to k and ΔL equal to the displacement x produced by the strain. This is truly the case for a deformed ideal (coiled) spring, of spring constant k, either compressed or elongated by an amount x. The relation between the force and deformation of the spring is well known. It is named Hooke's law of force after its discoverer and is written as:

$$F = -kx \tag{9}$$

The negative sign indicates the restoring nature of the force exerted by the spring when deformed. The frequency of vibration "f" of a mass–spring system (as shown below) is:

$$f = (1/2\pi)[m/k]^{1/2} \tag{10}$$

where m is the mass of the attached object and the spring mass is negligible.

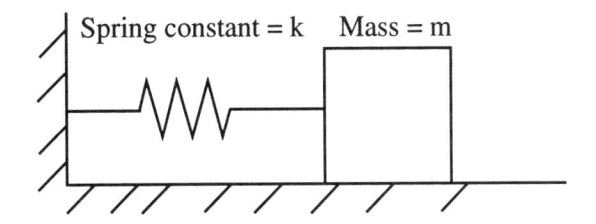

Test Yourself

1. Find the density and specific gravity of an alcohol if 75.0 g of it occupies 94.62 cm^3.

2. The nucleus of a hydrogen atom has a mass of 1.67×10^{-27} kg and a radius of 1.20×10^{-15} m. What is the density of the nucleus?

3. You can put 15 gallons of gasoline in the tank of a compact efficient car. The density of gasoline is 675 kg/m^3. What is the extra weight of the car due to this amount of gasoline? (1 gal = 3.785×10^{-3} m^3).

4. The density of cast iron is 7,200 kg/m^3. The dimension of the plate is 1.5 m × 1.0 m × 0.15 m. Find the mass and specific gravity of the armor plate (made of cast iron) placed to cover a manhole.

5. A piece of rock weighs 3.0 g in air, 1.7 g in water, and 0.8 g in an acid. Find the density and specific gravity of the acid.

6. An electrolytic copper-plating process uses 5.1 cm^3 of copper coating on each electronic

circuit board. How many similar circuit boards can be completely coated with 0.25 kg of silver? (Density of silver is 10.5×10^3 kg/m^3.)

7. One liter of milk containing 2% by volume butterfat weighs 1.021 kg. The density of butterfat is 865 kg/m^3.

   (a) How many grams of fat are there in a gallon of such milk?

   (b) What is the density of fat free skim milk?

8. A foam plastic (density 0.58 g/cc) is to be used as a lifeguard. What volume of plastic must be used to keep 25% (by volume) of a 95 kg person afloat? The average density of a person is 1.05 g/cm^3.

9. Atmospheric pressure is 1.01×10^5 Pa. How large is the force on the head of a person approximately 25 cm in diameter?

10. A submarine dives to a depth of 250 m below sea level. Find the pressure exerted on the exterior surface of the submarine. (Density of sea water is 1030 kg/m^3.)

11. A 100 kg antique solid statue lies at the bottom of a lake. It occupies a volume of 5×10^4 cm^3. How much force is needed to lift it up?

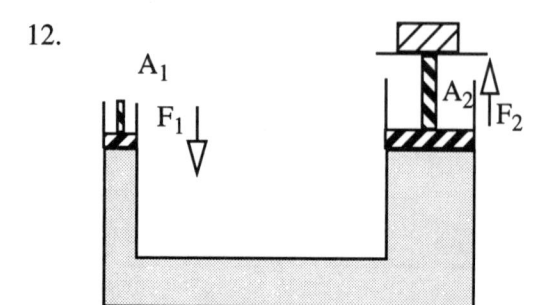

12.

In a car repair shop, the hydraulic press lifts a car of mass 2,500 kg by its larger piston (mass of piston = 50 kg) of cross-sectional area 8.5×10^{-2} m^2.

   (a) Find the force on the smaller piston of cross-sectional area 0.02 m^2.

   (b) Find the mechanical advantage.

13. A vertical tube has a 3 cm of oil (density 0.8 g/cm^3) floating on top of a 12 cm water column. What is the pressure at the bottom of the tube due to the weight of oil and water?

14. The density of ice is 917 kg/m^3. What fraction of the volume of ice will be above the water when floating in fresh water?

15. The pencil type tire pressure gauge shows 36 psi when attached to the tire valve of a truck. The spring of diameter 1 cm inside the instrument has a spring constant value of 550 N/m.

   (a) Find the absolute pressure in Pa in the tire.

   (b) How much will the spring be compressed? (1 psi = 6.89×10^3 Pa)

16. A 15 kg balloon has to lift a payload of 150 kg into the air. It is filled with helium gas of density 0.178 kg/m^3. The density of air is 1.29 kg/m^3. Find the volume of the balloon.

17. Water flows at a constant speed of 5 m/s through a pipe 12 cm in diameter for 30 minutes. How much water will be collected in a container placed at the exit end of the pipe?

18. 2.5 Liters of oil flow out of a tube of inner diameter 2.2 cm in 5 minutes. Find the average speed of the oil in the tube.

19. In a heartbeat, 80 mL of purified blood is pumped out of the heart through an artery of radius 0.5 cm. Find the average speed of the blood, assuming 65 heartbeats per minute.

20. What must be the gauge pressure of water at the exit end of a fire hoses held vertically up, to shoot the water 50 m high?

21. The gauge pressure in each of the four tires of a 1,500 kg car is 1.6 N/cm^2. How much area of each tire is in contact with the ground?

22. A horizontal pipe of diameter 5 cm has a constriction of diameter of 2.5 cm. The diameter of the pipe uniformly changes from a larger to a smaller value. The speed and pressure of the water at a point near the larger diameter are 4 m/s and 150 kPa. What are the speed and pressure at a point near the smaller diameter?

23. In the basement of a house, a hot water heating system uses a pipe that has a diameter of 6 cm. Water is circulated in this pipe at a speed of 0.75 m/s under a pressure of 4 atm. Calculate the flow speed and pressure of water in a pipe of diameter 3 cm placed on the second floor 8 m high.

24. Four identical columns of concrete equally support the weight of a building that has a mass of 250,000 kg. The area of cross section of each column is 1 m². Calculate the stress and strain in each column. (Young's modulus for concrete is 20×10^9 N/m².)

25. A 1.8 m long and 1mm diameter piano wire made of steel is designed to stretch up to 0.5 cm when musician plays on it. Find the strain and force on this wire. Young's modulus for steel is 2×10^{11} N/m².

26. A solid cylindrical steel column is 5 m long and 0.50 m in diameter. How much will the change in length be if it is used to support a load of 95,000 kg?

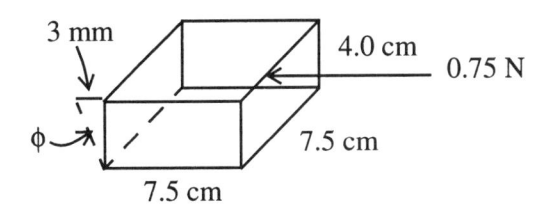

27.

A piece of Jell-O block (dimension 7.5 cm × 7.5 cm × 4.0 cm) sitting on a plate is pushed on its top surface with a horizontal force of 0.75 N. This results in displacing the top surface sideways by 3 mm while the bottom surface remains fixed to the plate. Find the shearing stress, shearing strain, and the shear modulus of Jell-O.

28. A 100 m tall building of dimension 20 m × 20 m at the base is designed to withstand a lateral maximum displacement of 1.5 m at the top. How large a shearing force can it sustain if an earthquake shakes the ground? Use a shear modulus for the building structure to be 8×10^{10} N/m.

29. A volume of 200 mL of water is subjected to a pressure of 1.75×10^7 Pa. How much will the volume contraction be if the bulk modulus of water is 1.7×10^9 N/m²?

30. A solid lead ball has a radius of 0.2 m in air. Bulk modulus of lead is 7.5×10^9 Pa. What will its radius be if taken to an ocean depth where the pressure is 1.5×10^8 Pa?

31. A large open-top tank is filled with water 5 m high. A hole 1.5 cm in diameter is opened at the bottom of the tank. What volume of water will escape per second?

32. A block of mass of 1.5 kg is attached to the free end of a vertical spring while the other end of the spring is held fixed. The mass vertically vibrates and undergoes simple harmonic motion with a frequency of 1.5 cycles/s. Find the spring constant. The mass of the spring is negligible.

33. In a children's park, the vertical coil spring under a rocking chair compresses 2.5 cm when a child of mass 30 kg sits on it.

    (a) What is the spring constant of the coil?
    (b) What will be the frequency of vibration of the spring if the child starts rocking up and down?

Check Yourself

1. Mass of alcohol = m = 75 g = 0.075 kg

    Volume of alcohol = V = 94.62 cm³ = 94.62×10^{-6} m³,   NOTE: 1 m³ = $(10^2)^3 = 1 \times 10^6$ cm³

    Density = $\dfrac{m}{V} = \dfrac{0.075}{94.62 \times 10^{-6}} = 792.6$ kg/m³

144 / Physics I

$$\text{sp gr} = \frac{\text{Density of alcohol}}{\text{Density of water}} = \frac{792.6}{1\times 10^3}$$

$$\text{sp gr} = 0.793 \quad \textbf{(Density)}$$

2. $$m = 1.67\times 10^{-27}\,\text{kg}$$

$$\text{Radius} = r = 1.20\times 10^{-15}\,\text{m}$$

$$\text{Volume of nucleus} = \frac{4}{3}\pi r^3 = \frac{4\pi \times (1.20\times 10^{-15})^3}{3}$$

$$V = 7.24\times 10^{-45}\,\text{m}^3$$

$$\text{Density} = \frac{m}{V} = \frac{1.67\times 10^{-27}}{7.24\times 10^{-45}}$$

$$\text{Density} = 2.31\times 10^{17}\,\text{kg/m}^3$$

(Density)

3. $$\text{Density} = \rho = \frac{m}{V}$$

$$m = \rho V$$

$$\rho = 675\,\text{kg/m}^3$$

$$V = 15\,\text{gal} = 15 \times 3.785\times 10^{-3}\,\text{m}^3 = 5.68\times 10^{-2}\,\text{m}^3$$

$$m = 675 \times 5.68\times 10^{-2} = 38.3\,\text{kg}$$

(Density)

4. $$\rho = 7200\,\text{kg/m}^3$$

$$\text{Volume} = V = 1.5 \times 1.0 \times 0.15 = 0.225\,\text{m}^3$$

$$m = \rho V = 7200 \times 0.225 = 1.62\times 10^3\,\text{kg}$$

$$\text{sp gr} = \frac{7200\,\text{kg/m}^3}{1\times 10^3\,\text{kg/m}^3}$$

$$\text{sp gr} = 7.2$$

(Density)

5. Volume of rock = volume of displaced water

Mass of displaced water = (3.0 − 1.7) = 1.3 g

So, volume of displaced water = 1.3 cm^3

Fluid Mechanics / 145

$V = 1.3 \text{ cm}^3 = 1.3 \times 10^{-6} \text{ m}^3$

Mass of displaced acid = $m = (3.0 - 0.8)$ g = 2.2 g = 2.2×10^{-3} kg

Density of the acid, $\rho = \dfrac{2.2 \times 10^{-3}}{1.3 \times 10^{-6}}$

$\rho = 1.69 \times 10^3 \text{ kg/m}^3$

$\text{sp gr} = \dfrac{\rho_{acid}}{\rho_{water}} = \dfrac{1.69 \times 10^3}{1.0 \times 10^3} = 1.69$

(Archimedes Principle)

6. V = Volume of copper/board = 5.1 cm^3 = 5.1×10^{-6} m^3

$\rho = \dfrac{m}{V}, \quad m = \rho V = 10.5 \times 10^3 \times 5.1 \times 10^{-6}$

$m = 5.3 \times 10^{-2}$ kg per board

Number of boards = $\dfrac{M}{m} = \dfrac{0.25}{5.3 \times 10^{-2}} = 4.72$

So, 4 such boards can be completely coated.

(Density)

7. 2% of one gallon = 0.02 gal

Volume of butterfat = $0.02 \times 3.785 \times 10^{-3} = 7.57 \times 10^{-5}$ m^3

Mass of butterfat = $\rho V = 865 \times 7.57 \times 10^{-5} = 6.55 \times 10^{-2}$ kg

$m = 65.5$ g in a gallon of 2% milk.

Mass of butter in one liter of 2% milk,

$m = \dfrac{6.55 \times 10^{-2} \text{ kg}}{1 \text{ gal}} \times \dfrac{1 \text{ gal}}{3.785 \text{ liter}} = 1.73 \times 10^{-2}$ kg

Therefore, volume of butterfat in a liter of 2% milk,

$V = 0.02$ L

Density of skim milk,

$\rho = \dfrac{m}{V} = \dfrac{(1.021 - 1.73 \times 10^{-2})}{(1 - 0.02)}$

$= \dfrac{1.004 \text{ kg}}{0.98 \times 10^{-3} \text{ m}^3}$

$\rho = 1024$ kg/m³

(Density)

8. Person: $\rho_p = 1.05$ g/cm³ $= \dfrac{1.05 \times 10^{-3} \text{ kg}}{1 \times 10^{-6} \text{ m}^3}$

   $\rho_p = 1.05 \times 10^3$ kg/m³

   $\rho_p = \dfrac{m}{V}, \quad V = \dfrac{m}{\rho_p} = \dfrac{95}{1.05 \times 10^3}$

   $V_p = 9.05 \times 10^{-2}$ m³

   Foam: $\rho_f = 0.58$ g/cc $= 5.8 \times 10^2$ kg/m³

   By condition of the problem,

   Volume of person inside water $= 0.75 \times 9.05 \times 10^{-2}$

   i.e., $V_{in} = 6.79 \times 10^{-2}$ m³ (inside water).

   Volume of displaced water $= 6.79 \times 10^{-2}$ m³

   Mass of displaced water $= 6.79 \times 10^{-2} \times 1 \times 10^3$ kg $= 67.9$ kg

   So,

   Mass of displaced water by man + Mass of displaced water by foam = Mass of man + Mass of foam.

   $67.9 + \rho_w V_f = 95 + \rho_f V_f$

   $(\rho_w - \rho_f) V_f = 95 - 67.9$

   $(1 \times 10^3 - 5.8 \times 10^2) V_f = 27.1$

   $4.2 \times 10^2 V_f = 27.1$

   $V_f = 6.45 \times 10^{-2}$ m³

   (Archimedes Principle)

9. $\dfrac{\text{Force}}{\text{Area}} = \text{Pressure}$

   $P = \dfrac{F}{A}, \quad F = PA$

So, $F = 1.01 \times 10^5 \times \pi \times \left(\frac{0.25}{2}\right)^2$

$F = 4.96 \times 10^3$ N

(Force/pressure)

10. P = Pressure of atmosphere + pressure of water column

$P = P_{atm} + \rho g h$

$= 1.01 \times 10^5 + 1030 \times 9.8 \times 250$

$= 1.01 \times 10^5 + 2.52 \times 10^6$

$P = 2.62 \times 10^6$ Pa

(Force/pressure)

11.   Mass of displaced water = 5×10^4 cm^3 × 1 g/cc

$= 5 \times 10^4$ g = 50 kg

Buoyant Force = $50 \times 9.8 = 490$ N

Force of gravity on statue = $mg = 100 \times 9.8$

$F_g = 9.8 \times 10^2$ N

Force Needed = $F_g - F_b = 980 - 490$

$= 490$ N

(Archimedes Principle)

12.

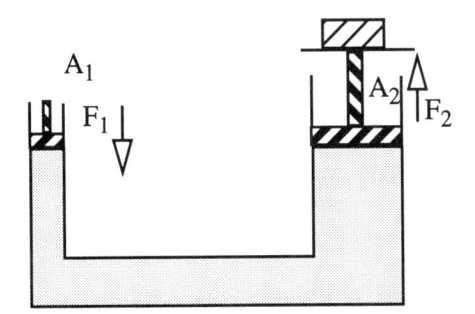

(a) Pressure on each column must be the same by Pascal's Principle.

$P_1 = P_2$

$\dfrac{F_1}{A_1} = \dfrac{F_2}{A_2}$

148 / Physics I

$$F_1 = \frac{F_2}{A_2}A_1 = \frac{(2500 + 50) \times 9.8 \times 0.02}{8.5 \times 10^{-2}}$$

$$F_1 = 5.88 \times 10^3 \text{ N}$$

(b) Mechanical Advantage $= \dfrac{F_2}{F_1} = \dfrac{2550 \times 9.8}{5.88 \times 10^3} = 4.25$

(Pascal's Principle)

13. $P = P_{water} + P_{oil}$

$= \rho_w g h_1 + \rho_o g h_2$

$= 1 \times 10^3 \times 9.8 \times 0.12 + 0.8 \times 10^3 \times 9.8 \times 0.03$

$= 1.176 \times 10^3 + 0.235 \times 10^3$

$P = 1.41 \times 10^3 \text{ Pa}$

(Force/pressure)

14. Weight of displaced water = Weight of ice

$\rho_w g V_w = \rho_i g V_i$

$\dfrac{V_w}{V_i} = \dfrac{\rho_i}{\rho_w}$

$\dfrac{V_i - V_w}{V_i} = \dfrac{\rho_w - \rho_i}{\rho_w}$

$\dfrac{\Delta V}{V} = \dfrac{1 \times 10^3 - 917}{1 \times 10^3} = \dfrac{83}{1000} = 0.083$

So, 8.3% of volume of ice is above water.

(Archimedes Principle)

15. Absolute Pressure = Gauge Pressure + Atmospheric Pressure

$$P = P_g + P_a$$

(a) $P = 36 \times 6.89 \times 10^3 + 1.01 \times 10^5$

$P = 3.49 \times 10^5 \text{ Pa}$

(Force/pressure)

(b) Force on the spring due to air pressure is:

$$F = PA = (3.49 \times 10^5)[\pi \times (0.5 \times 10^{-2})^2]$$

$$F = 27.4 \text{ N}$$

From Hooke's law, $F = kx$

Therefore, $kx = 27.4$

$$550x = 27.4$$

$$x = 4.98 \times 10^{-2} \text{ m}$$

$$x = 4.98 \text{ cm}$$

(Simple harmonic motion)

16. Here, the buoyant force F = Weight of displaced air = Weight of payload + Weight of balloon + Weight of helium

$$\rho_{air} Vg = (150 + 15)g + \rho_{He} Vg$$

$$V(\rho_{air} - \rho_{He}) = 165$$

$$V(1.29 - 0.178) = 165$$

$$V = \frac{165}{1.112} = 148.4 \text{ m}^3$$

(Archimedes Principle)

17. Area of cross-section = $\pi r^2 = \pi(6 \times 10^{-2})^2$

$$A = 1.13 \times 10^{-2} \text{ m}^2$$

Flow rate = $Av = (1.13 \times 10^{-2} \times 5) = 5.65 \times 10^{-2} \text{ m}^3/\text{s}$

Volume of water collected,

$$V = Avt = (5.65 \times 10^{-2})(30 \times 60)$$

$$V = 1.02 \times 10^2 \text{ m}^3$$

(Equation of continuity)

18. $V = 2.5 \text{ L} = 2.5 \times 10^3 \text{ cm}^3 = 2.5 \times 10^{-3} \text{ m}^3$

$$A = \pi r^2 = \pi(1.1 \times 10^{-2})^2 = 3.80 \times 10^{-4} \text{ m}^2$$

$$V = Avt$$

$$2.5 \times 10^{-3} = 3.8 \times 10^{-4} \times v \times 5 \times 60$$

$$v = 2.19 \times 10^{-2} \text{ m/s}$$

$$v = 2.19 \text{ cm/s average speed}$$

(Equation of continuity)

19. $t = \dfrac{60}{65} = 0.923 s$

$A = \pi r^2 = \pi(0.5 \times 10^{-2})^2 = 7.85 \times 10^{-5} \text{ m}^2$

$V = 80 \text{ mL} = 80 \text{ cm}^3 = 80 \times 10^{-6} = 8.0 \times 10^{-5} \text{ m}^3$

$V = Avt$

$v = \dfrac{V}{tA} = \dfrac{8 \times 10^{-5}}{(0.923)(7.85 \times 10^{-5})}$

$v = 1.1 \text{ m/s}$

(Equation of continuity)

20. $v^2 = v_0^2 - 2gh$

$0 = v_o^2 - 2gh$

$v_o = \sqrt{2gh} = [2 \times 9.8 \times 50]^{\frac{1}{2}} = 31.3$

$v_o = 31.3 \text{ m/s}$

Using Bernoulli's Equation, for points just inside and just outside the exit end we have,

$$P_{in} + \dfrac{1}{2}\rho v_{in}^2 + \rho g h_{in} = P_{out} + \dfrac{1}{2}\rho v_{out}^2 + \rho g h_{out}$$

Here, $\quad h_{in} \approx h_{out}$

$v_{in} \approx 0$

$P_{in} - P_{out} = \dfrac{1}{2}\rho v_{out}^2 = \dfrac{1}{2}\rho(\sqrt{2gh})^2$

$= \dfrac{1}{2}\rho(2gh)$

$= \rho g h = (1 \times 10^3) \times 9.8 \times 50$

Gauge Pressure $= 4.9 \times 10^5$ Pa $= 490$ kPa

(Bernoulli's Equation)

21. Weight of car = $1500 \times 9.8 = 1.47 \times 10^4$ N

Force on each tire = $\dfrac{1.47 \times 10^4}{4} = 3.675 \times 10^3$ N

$$P = \dfrac{F}{A}$$

So, $F = PA = (P_g + P_a)A$

$$A = \dfrac{F}{P_g + P_a} = \dfrac{3.675 \times 10^3 \text{ N}}{(1.6 \times 10^4 \times 1.01 \times 10^5) \text{ N/m}^2}$$

$$A = \dfrac{3.675 \times 10^3}{1.17 \times 10^5} = 3.14 \times 10^{-2} \text{ m}^2$$

$A = 314 \text{ cm}^2$

(Force/pressure)

22. Using Bernoulli's Equation,

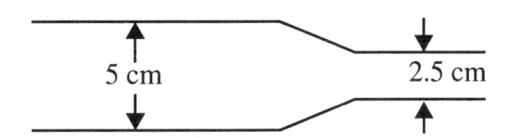

$$P_1 + \rho g h_1 + \dfrac{1}{2}\rho v_1^2 = P_2 + \rho g h_2 + \dfrac{1}{2}\rho v_2^2$$

$h_1 = h_2$

$$P_1 - P_2 = \dfrac{1}{2}\rho(v_2^2 - v_1^2) \qquad (1)$$

From the equation of continuity,

$A_1 v_1 = A_2 v_2$

$$v_2 = \left(\dfrac{A_1 v_1}{A_2}\right) = \dfrac{\pi r_1^2 v_1}{\pi r_2^2} = \left(\dfrac{r_1}{r_2}\right)^2 v_1$$

$$v_2 = \left(\dfrac{5}{2.5}\right)^2 (4) = 16 \text{ m/s}$$

$v_2 = 16$ m/s at smaller diameter

From equation (1),

$$150\times10^3 - P_2 = \frac{1}{2}(1\times10^3)(16^2 - 4^2)$$

$$P_2 = 1.5\times10^5 - 1.2\times10^5$$

$$P_2 = 0.3\times10^5$$

$$P_2 = 30 \text{ kPa}$$

(Bernoulli's Equation)

23. From the equation of continuity we have,

$$\rho_1 A_1 v_1 = \rho_2 A_2 v_2$$

$$\rho_1 = \rho_2$$

$$A_1 v_1 = A_2 v_2$$

$$v_2 = \frac{A_1 v_1}{A_2} = \left(\frac{6}{3}\right)^2 (0.75) = 4 \times 0.75$$

$$v_2 = 3 \text{ m/s}$$

$$P_1 + \rho g h_1 + \frac{1}{2}\rho v_1^2 = P_2 + \rho g h_2 + \frac{1}{2}\rho v_2^2$$

$$P_1 - P_2 = \rho g(h_2 - h_1) + \frac{1}{2}\rho(v_2^2 - v_1^2)$$

$$= \rho\left[g(h_2 - h_1) + \frac{v_2^2 - v_1^2}{2}\right]$$

$$= 1\times10^3[9.8(8) + 0.5(3^2 - 0.75^2)]$$

$$= 1000[78.4 + 4.22]$$

$$P_1 - P_2 = 8.26 \times 10^4, \quad P_1 = 4 \text{ atm}$$

$$P_2 = 4 \times 1.013\times10^5 - 8.26\times10^4$$

$$= 4.052\times10^5 - 8.26\times10^4$$

$$P_2 = 3.23\times10^5 \text{ Pa}$$

(Bernoulli's Equation)

Fluid Mechanics / 153

24. Weight of the building = $2.5 \times 10^5 \times 9.8$

$$= 2.45 \times 10^6 \text{ N}$$

Force on each column = $2.45 \times 10^6 / 4$

$$= 6.125 \times 10^5 \text{ N}$$

$$\text{Stress} = \frac{F}{A} = \frac{6.125 \times 10^5}{1} = 6.125 \times 10^5 \text{ N/m}^2$$

$$\text{Young's Modulus} = Y = \frac{\text{Stress}}{\text{Strain}}$$

$$\text{Strain} = \frac{\text{Stress}}{Y} = \frac{6.12 \times 10^5}{2 \times 10^{10}}$$

$$\text{Strain} = 3.06 \times 10^{-5}$$

(Elasticity)

25. $\text{Strain} = \frac{\Delta L}{L} = \frac{0.5 \times 10^{-2}}{1.8} = 2.78 \times 10^{-3}$

$$Y = \frac{\text{Stress}}{\text{Strain}}$$

$$\text{Stress} = Y(\text{Strain}) = 2 \times 10^{11} \times 2.78 \times 10^{-3}$$

$$= 5.56 \times 10^8 \text{ N/m}^2$$

$\text{Stress} = \frac{F}{A}$, $F = A(\text{Stress})$

$F = \pi r^2 (\text{Stress}) = \pi (0.001)^2 (5.56 \times 10^8)$

$F = 1.74 \times 10^3 \text{ N}$

(Elasticity)

26. $Y = 2 \times 10^{11} \text{ N/m}^2$ for steel

$A = \pi r^2 = \pi (0.25)^2 = 1.96 \times 10^{-1} \text{ m}^2$

Force = $95000 \times 9.8 = 9.31 \times 10^5 \text{ N}$

$\text{Stress} = \frac{F}{A} = \frac{9.31 \times 10^5}{1.96 \times 10^{-1}} = 4.75 \times 10^6 \text{ N/m}^2$

$$Y = \frac{\text{Stress}}{\text{Strain}}$$

$$\text{Strain} = \frac{\text{Stress}}{Y}$$

$$\frac{\Delta L}{L} = \frac{4.75 \times 10^6}{2 \times 10^{11}} = 2.37 \times 10^{-5}$$

$$\Delta L = L(\text{Strain}) = 5(2.37 \times 10^{-5})$$

$$\Delta L = 1.19 \times 10^{-4} \text{ m} = 0.12 \text{ mm}$$

(Elasticity)

27. $\text{Strain} = (\Delta L)/h = \dfrac{3 \times 10^{-3}}{4 \times 10^{-2}} = 0.75 \times 10^{-1}$

    $\text{Strain} = \tan\phi = 0.075$ (For small angle $\tan\phi \approx \phi$)

    $$\text{Shearing Modulus} = \frac{F}{A \tan\phi} = \frac{0.75}{(7.5 \times 10^{-2})^2 (0.75 \times 10^{-1})}$$

    $$= 1.78 \times 10^3 \text{ N/m}^2$$

    $\text{Shearing Stress} = 1.78 \times 10^3 \times 0.075 = 1.33 \times 10^2 \text{ N/m}^2$

(Elasticity)

28. $\text{Strain} = \dfrac{\text{Lateral displacement}}{\text{Height}} = \dfrac{1.5}{100} = 1.5 \times 10^{-2}$

    $\text{Shearing modulus}, S = \dfrac{\text{Stress}}{\text{Strain}}$

    $\text{Stress} = (S)\, \text{Strain} = (8 \times 10^{10}) \times (1.5 \times 10^{-2}) \text{ N/m}^2$

    $\text{Stress} = \dfrac{\text{Force}}{\text{Area}} = 1.2 \times 10^9 \text{ N/m}^2$

    $\text{Force}, F = 1.2 \times 10^9 \times A$

    $\qquad\qquad = 1.2 \times 10^9 \times (20 \times 20)$

    $\qquad\qquad = 1.2 \times 4 \times 10^{11}$

    $\qquad F = 4.8 \times 10^{11} \text{ N}$

(Elasticity)

29. $\text{Stress} = \dfrac{\text{Force}}{\text{Area}} = 1.75 \times 10^7$ Pa, $V = 200$ mL

$\text{Strain} = \dfrac{\Delta V}{V} = \dfrac{\Delta V}{200 \times (10^{-2})^3} = \dfrac{\Delta V}{2 \times 10^{-4}}$

Bulk Modulus,

$$B = \dfrac{\text{Stress}}{\text{Strain}} = \dfrac{1.75 \times 10^7}{\dfrac{\Delta V}{V}} = \dfrac{1.75 \times 10^7 \times 2 \times 10^{-4}}{\Delta V}$$

$1.7 \times 10^9 = \dfrac{3.5 \times 10^3}{\Delta V}$

$\Delta V = \dfrac{3.5 \times 10^3}{1.7 \times 10^9} = 2.06 \times 10^{-6}$ m^3

$\Delta V = 2.06$ mL **(Elasticity)**

30. $\text{Stress} = \dfrac{\text{Force}}{\text{Area}} = 1.5 \times 10^8$ Pa

Bulk Modulus, $B = \dfrac{\text{Stress}}{\text{Strain}}$

$7.5 \times 10^9 = \dfrac{1.5 \times 10^8}{\text{Strain}}$

$\text{Strain} = \dfrac{1.5 \times 10^8}{7.5 \times 10^9} = 2 \times 10^{-2}$

$\dfrac{\Delta V}{V} = 2 \times 10^{-2}$ \hfill (1)

$\Delta V = \dfrac{4\pi}{3} r_0^3 - \dfrac{4\pi}{3} r^3 = \dfrac{4\pi}{3}(r_o^3 - r^3)$

$\Delta V = \dfrac{4\pi}{3}(r_0 - r)(r_0^2 + r_o r + r^2)$

$\Delta V \cong \dfrac{4\pi}{3}(\Delta r) 3 r_o^2$ (since $r \approx r_0$)

$\dfrac{\Delta V}{V} = \dfrac{(4\pi/3)(\Delta r_0) 3 r_0^2}{(4\pi/3) r_0^3} = \dfrac{3(\Delta r)}{r_0}$

Using equation (1),

$$2\times 10^{-2} = \left(\frac{3}{r_0}\right)\Delta r$$

$$\Delta r = \frac{2\times 10^{-2} \times 0.2}{3} = 1.33\times 10^{-3} \text{ m}$$

$$r = r_o - \Delta r = 0.2 - 1.33\times 10^{-3} = 0.199$$

So, new radius is 0.199 m

(Elasticity)

31.

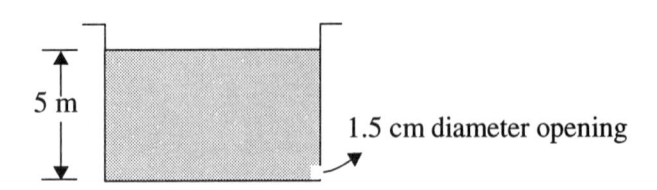

From Bernoulli's Equation,

$$P_1 + \frac{1}{2}\rho v_1^2 + h_1\rho g = P_2 + \frac{1}{2}\rho v + h_2\rho g$$

Here speed inside, $v_1 = 0$, $P_1 = P_2$ and $h_1 = 5$ m

$$h_2 = 0,$$

$$\frac{1}{2}\rho v_2^2 = \rho g(h_1 - h_2)$$

$$v_2 = \sqrt{2g(h_1 - h_2)} = [2\times 9.8 \times 5]^{\frac{1}{2}} = 9.9 \text{ m/s}$$

Rate of flow,

$$A_2 v_2 = \pi r^2 v_2 = \pi(0.75\times 10^{-2})^2 9.9$$

$$= 1.75\times 10^{-3} \text{ m}^3/\text{s}$$

(Bernoulli's Equation)

32.

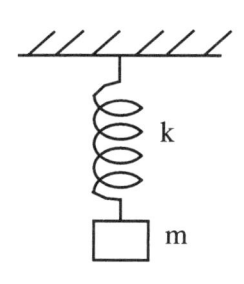

$$f = \frac{1}{2\pi}\sqrt{\frac{k}{m}}$$

$$f^2 = \frac{1}{4\pi^2}\left(\frac{k}{m}\right)$$

$$k = 4\pi^2 f^2 m = 4\pi^2 \times (1.5)^2 1.5 = 1.33 \times 10^2$$

$$k = 133 \text{ N/m}$$

(Simple harmonic motion)

33.

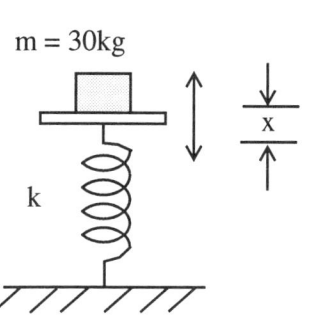

$m = 30$ kg

$x = 2.5$ cm $= 2.5 \times 10^{-2}$ m

(a) $F = -kx$

$$k = \left|\frac{F}{x}\right| = \frac{mg}{x}$$

$$k = \frac{30 \times 9.8}{2.5 \times 10^{-2}} = 1.18 \times 10^4$$

$$k = 1.18 \times 10^4 \text{ N/m}$$

(b) $f = \dfrac{1}{2\pi}\sqrt{\dfrac{k}{m}} = \dfrac{1}{2\pi}\left(\dfrac{1.18 \times 10^4}{30}\right)^{\frac{1}{2}}$

$f = 3.15$ cycles/sec.

(Simple harmonic motion)

Grade Yourself

Circle the question numbers that you had incorrect. Then indicate the number of questions you missed. If you answered more than three questions incorrectly, you need to focus on that topic. (If a topic has less than three questions and you had at least one wrong, we suggest you study that topic also. Read your textbook, a review book, or ask your teacher for help.)

Subject: Fluid Mechanics

Topic	Question Numbers	Number Incorrect
Density	1, 2, 3, 4, 6, 7	
Archimedes Principle	5, 8, 11, 14, 16	
Force/pressure	9, 10, 13, 15(a), 21	
Pascal's Principle	12	
Equation of continuity	17, 18, 19	
Bernoulli's Equation	20, 22, 23, 31	
Elasticity	24, 25, 26, 27, 28, 29, 30	
Simple harmonic motion	15(b), 32, 33	

Temperature, Heat, and Thermodynamics

11

Brief Yourself

Temperature:

A thermometer is used to measure temperature. There are two common types of temperature scales, Fahrenheit (°F) and Celsius (°C) (also known as Centigrade). The temperature difference between the freezing and boiling points of water is divided into 100 parts in the Celsius scale and 180 parts in the Fahrenheit scale. The freezing point of water is 0 on the Celsius scale and 32 on the Fahrenheit scale. Hence, the relation between the two temperature scales is:

$$T_C/100 = (T_F - 32)/180 \qquad (1)$$

where T_C is the temperature in Celsius and T_F in Fahrenheit. If you know one, you can find the other from equation (1).

Another temperature scale used in the scientific community is the Kelvin scale (°K), named in honor of Lord Kelvin. The relation between the Celsius and Kelvin scales of temperature is:

$$T_K = T_C + 273.15 \qquad (2)$$

where T_K is temperature on the Kelvin scale, also known as the absolute scale.

Thermal Expansion:

Material bodies generally expand when their temperature is raised. The known relation for the thermal expansion of a solid is:

$$L - L_0 = \alpha L_0 (T - T_0) \qquad (3)$$

where, L and L_0 are lengths of the solid at temperatures T and T_0. The constant α is called the coefficient of linear expansion.

Similarly, when a volume (V_0) of a gas expands or contracts due to a change in its temperature, we have the relation:

$$V - V_0 = \beta V_0 (T - T_0) \qquad (4)$$

where β is the coefficient of volume expansion.

Specific Heat:

Heat (denoted by Q), a form of energy, always flows from a hotter body to a colder one. The amount of heat energy (ΔQ) absorbed by a cold body or flowing out of a hot body is proportional to the temperature difference (ΔT) between the two bodies.

$$\Delta Q = c(m)(\Delta T) \tag{5}$$

where c is the specific heat and m the mass of the body absorbing or giving out heat. Conservation of energy, a law of physics, demands that the heat flowing out of the hot body must be equal to the heat absorbed by the other.

Heat Transfer:

There are three different ways in which heat flows from one body to another. These are conduction, convection, and radiation.

Conduction: Whenever heat energy is transferred from a hotter body to a colder body by the vibration of atoms and molecules about equilibrium positions, without actual transport of these atoms and molecules, the process is known as heat conduction. The time rate of heat transferred by conduction through an area of cross-section A between two points separated by a distance Δx and having a temperature difference of ΔT is:

$$\Delta Q/\Delta t = kA(\Delta T/\Delta x) \tag{6}$$

where k is the coefficient of thermal conductivity and (ΔT/Δx) is called the temperature gradient.

When there are N number of adjacent walls of the same area A, heat flow by conduction, for a difference in temperature ΔT, is:

$$\Delta Q/\Delta t = A(\Delta T)/[(\Delta x_1/k_1) + (\Delta x_2/k_2) + \ldots\ldots + (\Delta x_N/k_N)]$$

where Δx represents thickness and k represents thermal conductivity.

Convection: In liquids and gases, the atoms and molecules move from regions of higher temperature to regions of lower temperature by actual transport from one to another place. This process of heat transfer is called heat convection. If a fluid current moves over a surface area A during a time Δt, then the heat transfer per unit time by convection is:

$$\Delta Q/\Delta t = hA(\Delta T) \tag{7}$$

where h is the coefficient of heat convection and ΔT is the temperature difference between the surface and the moving fluid.

Radiation: Heat transfer by radiation occurs when a body emits electromagnetic waves into the surrounding space. The time rate of heat energy transferred by radiation from a hot body having surface area A at temperature T into the surrounding space at temperature T' is given by the Stefan-Boltzmann law:

$$\Delta Q/\Delta t = \varepsilon \sigma A(T^4 - T'^4) \tag{8}$$

where ε is the emissivity of the body and $\sigma = 5.67 \times 10^{-8}$ (W/m^2)K^4 is called the Stefan-Boltzmann constant.

Thermodynamics:

A small amount of work (ΔW) is done when a body at constant pressure p, expands by a small volume (ΔV). We may write,

$$\Delta W = p\Delta V \tag{9}$$

According to the First Law of Thermodynamics, heat (ΔQ) flowing into a system can be partly used to increase its internal energy (ΔU) and partly used to do work by the system, but the sum must be constant. The law may be expressed as:

$$\Delta Q = \Delta U + \Delta W \tag{10}$$

The internal energy of an ideal gas changes only if its temperature is changed. In processes at constant temperature, called isothermal processes, the internal energy of an ideal gas does not change. In addition, if the pressure remains constant in an isothermal process, then:

$$\Delta Q = \Delta W = p\Delta V \tag{11}$$

For an ideal gas that changes from (p_1, V_1) to (p_2, V_2) in an isothermal process:

$$\Delta Q = \Delta W = (p_1 V_1)\ln(V_2/V_1) \tag{12}$$

When no heat is added or taken out from a system, the process is called an adiabatic process. In adiabatic process, work is done at the expense of internal energy. So:

$$\Delta W = -\Delta U$$

For an ideal gas changing from (p_1, V_1, T_1) to (p_2, V_2, T_2) in an adiabatic process:

$$p_1(V_1)^\gamma = p_2(V_2)^\gamma$$

and, $T_1(V_1)^{\gamma-1} = T_2(V_2)^{\gamma-1}$

where gamma (γ) is the ratio of specific heats at constant pressure and at constant volume.

According to the Second Law of Thermodynamics, heat always flows from a hot reservoir to a cold reservoir and the reverse process does not occur in nature. The reverse process can only occur with application of some kind of external work. When a system changes from one equilibrium state to another through a series of small increments, it is called a reversible process. Entropy (S) is a variable of a system just like p, V, or T. When a system changes from one equilibrium state to another along a *reversible path*, heat ΔQ flowing into the system at absolute temperature T changes the entropy as:

$$\Delta S = \Delta Q/T \tag{13}$$

For an ideal engine operating between temperature T_1 and T_2 ($T_1 > T_2$) in a reversible process, the efficiency is given by:

$$e = (1 - T_2/T_1) \tag{14}$$

Test Yourself

1. On a cold day, you measure the outside temperature to be –15°F. What is the temperature in Celsius scale?

2. A radio station broadcasts the outside temperature to be –3°C. What will be the temperature in Fahrenheit and Kelvin?

3. A 50 cm long thin iron rod at 15°C is heated to 155°C. Find the increase in length. The coefficient of linear expansion of iron is 1.2×10^{-5} °C^{-1}.

4. A cylinder of radius 1.5 cm is to be slid into a copper pipe of inner radius 1.4995 cm. The radii were taken at the same temperature. The coefficient of linear expansion of copper is 1.7×10^{-5} °C^{-1}. Find the increase in temperature of the copper pipe needed in order to slide in the cylinder. Assume that expansion of the diameters is linear in temperature.

5. A steel meter ruler is calibrated at 20°C. The coefficient of linear expansion of steel is 1.1×10^{-5} °C^{-1}. What will be the percent error in using it at –25°C?

6. Calculate the increase in volume of 500 c.c. of mercury if the temperature is raised from 22°C to 95°C. The coefficient of volume expansion for mercury is 0.00018/°C.

7. An alloy of mass 225 g is heated to 550°C. It is then quickly placed in 450 g of water at 12°C. The water is contained in an aluminum calorimeter cup of mass 210 g. The final temperature of the mixture is 31.7°C. Specific heat of aluminum is 0.215 cal/g°C. Find the specific heat of the alloy.

8. The density of gold is 19.35 g/cm^3 at 20°C. Find the density of the same gold at 80°C. The coefficient of linear expansion of gold is 1.43×10^{-5} °C^{-1}.

9. How much heat is required to convert 2.5 g of ice at –15°C into steam at 135°C? Specific heats of ice = 0.5 cal/g°C, water = 1.0 cal/g°C, and steam = 0.481 cal/g°C. The latent heat of fusion for water is 80 cal/g and the latent heat of vaporization is 540 cal/g.

10. After a snow storm, your driveway of area 50 m^2 is covered with a layer of ice 10 cm high at a temperature of 0°C. You decide to use sunlight falling at 200 W/m^2 to melt the ice. How long will it take to melt all the ice? Is it a good idea? (Density of ice is 920 kg/m^3 and 1 cal = 4.184 J.)

11. In a physics experiment, 250 g of water is placed in a 50 g calorimeter cup made of aluminum when both are at 15°C. Steam at 100°C is completely absorbed by passing it through the water, raising the temperature of water and cup to 45°C. Find the mass of steam absorbed. Specific heat of aluminum is 0.215 cal/g °C.

12. A 100 W incandescent lamp of filament area 45 mm^2, emits all its energy by radiation into the surrounding space of the room at 22°C. If the filament emissivity is 0.32, find the temperature of the filament.

13. Heat energy leaks through a small hole (of area 1.2 cm^2) in a furnace at 2,100°C into the surrounding atmosphere at 24°C. What is the rate of heat loss through this hole? The emissivity of the furnace is 1.

14. In a double-pane window made of two glass plates, a layer of stagnant air 0.3 cm wide separates the two plates. The dimension of each glass plate is 75 cm × 95 cm × 0.3 cm. In a cold night, the indoor surface temperature of the glass plate is 23°C while the outdoor surface temperature of the glass plate is –15°C. Thermal conductivity of glass and air are 0.84 W/m°C and 0.08 W/m°C, respectively. What is the rate of heat loss through the glass of this window?

15. The walls of a house are insulated with a 15 cm thick layer of glass wool placed inside the wall. How thick should a concrete wall be if the same amount of insulation as is provided by the glass wool is required? Thermal conductivity of glass

wool and concrete are 4.14×10^{-2} W/m°C and 1.3 W/m°C, respectively.

16. On a hot summer day, the air current from a fan takes away 12 J/m²s°C from the unclothed part of the body having area 1.5 m². The difference in temperature between your body and the surroundings is 10°C. How much convective heat loss in kcal/h can you enjoy due to only the fan? Assume the heat loss in still air to be 90 kcal/h.

17. In a daily routine, the work done by a 70 kg person may be divided into 8 h of sleeping (60 kcal/h), 5 h of walking (moderate physical labor, 400 kcal/h), 3 h of eating and dressing (light activity, 200 kcal/h), and the rest of the time in relaxing or being busy at a desk (100 kcal/h). Assume all of the heat energy comes from taking 4,500 kcal of food daily.

    (a) How much is the daily change in the internal energy of the body?
    (b) How long must the person exercise (1,000 kcal/h), at the expense of relaxation, in order to avoid body fat?

18. A mass of 75 kg of water at 15°C is heated to 25°C. What is the change in the internal energy of this water?

19. A vertical spring (k = 450 N/m) supports a mass of 0.75 kg made of lead (sp. ht = 0.038 J/kg°C). The block vibrates inside 1.2 kg of water when the spring is compressed by 0.45 m and released. How much is the change of water temperature when the mass stops and thermal equilibrium is reached?

20. A motor supplies 1.5 hp to a water-wheel immersed in 10 gal of water in a humidifier. The water temperature changes by 0.02°C due to heating by friction that uses 20% of the power delivered by the motor.

    (a) How much is the change in the internal energy of the water?
    (b) How long will it take?

21. The temperature of 0.15 kg of helium gas is raised from 18°C to 155°C at constant pressure. Find the change in internal energy of the gas and the external work done by the gas. (For He, c_v = 0.75 kcal/kg°K and c_p = 1.15 kcal/kg°K)

22. Water of mass 0.2 kg at 100°C is converted into steam at 100°C in a reversible process. How much is the change in entropy of the water?

23. A steam engine operates between 500°C and 150°C. Find the highest efficiency achievable in this engine.

24. A car engine operates between temperatures of 550°C and 1,650°C. It uses one gallon of gasoline to produce a total work of 6×10^8 J. The density of gasoline is 680 kg/m³ and it produces 4.8×10^7 J/kg at combustion. Find the efficiency of Carnot's ideal engine and this engine.

25. Starting at normal temperature and pressure, 5kg of an ideal gas (M = 28 kg/kmol) is compressed to one quarter of its initial volume while keeping its temperature constant. What is the change in the entropy of the gas?

Check Yourself

1. Temperature in Fahrenheit, $T_F = -15°F$

$$\frac{T_C}{100} = \frac{T_F - 32}{180}$$

$$T_C = 100 \times \frac{T_F - 32}{180}$$

$$= \frac{100 \times (-15 - 32)}{180}$$

$$= -\frac{100 \times 47}{180}$$

$$= -26.1$$

Temperature in Celsius, $T_C = -26.1°C$

(Temperature)

2. $\quad \dfrac{T_C}{100} = \dfrac{T_F - 32}{180}$

$\dfrac{-3}{100} = \dfrac{T_F - 32}{180}$

$T_F - 32 = -180 \times \dfrac{3}{100}$

$T_F = 32 - 5.4$

$T_F = 26.6° F$

Temperature in Kelvin Scale is,

$T_K = T_C + 273 = -3 + 273 = 270$

$T_K = 270° K$

(Temperature)

3. $\quad L_o = 0.50$ m

$T_o = 15°C$

$T = 155°C$

$\alpha = 1.2 \times 10^{-5} °C^{-1}$

$L - L_o = \alpha L_o (T - T_o)$

$= 1.2 \times 10^{-5} \times 0.5 \times (155 - 15)$

$= 1.2 \times 0.5 \times 140 \times 10^{-5}$

$= 8.4 \times 10^{-4} = 0.84 \times 10^{-3}$

$\Delta L = (L - L_o) = 0.84$ mm is the increase in length.

(Thermal expansion)

4.

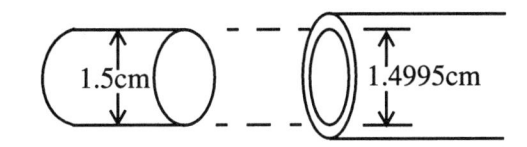

$L_0 = 1.4995 \times 10^{-2}$ m

$L = 1.5 \times 10^{-2}$ m

$\alpha = 1.7 \times 10^{-5}$ per °C for copper.

$L - L_0 = \alpha L_0 (T - T_0)$

$(T - T_0) = \dfrac{L - L_0}{\alpha L_0} = \dfrac{(1.5 - 1.4995) \times 10^{-2}}{1.7 \times 10^{-5} \times 1.4995 \times 10^{-2}}$

$\Delta T = 19.6°$ C is the required increase in temperature.

(Thermal expansion)

5. $L_0 = 1$ m

$T_0 = 20°$ C

$T = -25°$ C

$\alpha = 1.1 \times 10^{-5}$ °C^{-1}

$L - L_0 = \alpha L_0 (T - T_0)$

$\dfrac{L - L_0}{L_0} = \alpha (T - T_0)$

$= 1.1 \times 10^{-5} (-25 - 20)$

$= 1.1 \times 10^{-5} (-45)$

$= 4.95 \times 10^{-4}$

% change in length,

$\dfrac{L - L_0}{L_0} \times 100 = -4.95 \times 10^{-4} \times 100 = -4.95 \times 10^{-2} = -0.0495$

Percent error is 0.05%.

(Thermal expansion)

6. $V - V_o = \beta V_o(T - T_o)$

$$\Delta V = 500 \text{ cm}^3 \times 0.00018(°C^{-1})(95-22)°C$$

$$= (500 \times 10^{-6} \text{ m}^3)(0.00018)(73)$$

$$= 6.57 \times 10^{-6} \text{ m}^3$$

$\Delta V = 6.57 \text{ cm}^3$ increase in volume

(Thermal expansion)

7. Heat absorbed = Heat given off

$$M_w C_w(T_f - T_i) + M_c C_c(T_f - T_i) = M_a C_a(T_i - T_f)$$

$$450 \times 1 \times (31.7 - 12) + 210 \times 0.215(31.7 - 12) = 225 \times C_a \times (550 - 31.7)$$

$$450 \times 19.7 + 210 \times 0.215 \times 19.7 = 225 \times 518.3 \ C_a$$

$$C_a = \frac{8.865 \times 10^3 + 8.894 \times 10^2}{1.166 \times 10^5}$$

$C_a = 0.084°$ cal/g°C is the specific heat of an alloy.

(Heat)

8. $\rho = \dfrac{m}{V}, \quad \rho V = m = $ constant

$$\rho_o V_o = \rho V$$

$$\rho_o V_o = \rho V_o[1 + 3\alpha(T - T_o)]$$

$$\rho = \frac{\rho_o}{1 + 3\alpha(T - T_o)} = \frac{19.35}{1 + 3 \times 1.43 \times 10^5 \times (80 - 20)}$$

$$\rho = \frac{19.35}{1 + 2.574 \times 10^{-3}} = 19.3 \text{ g/cm}^3$$

(Thermal expansion)

9. Heat given off = Heat absorbed.

Heat absorbed = $M_i C_i(15) + M_i L_f + M_w C_w(100) + M_w L_v + M_s C_s(35)$

$$= 2.5 \times 0.5 \times 15 + 2.5 \times 80 + 2.5 \times 1 \times 100 + 2.5 \times 540 + 2.5 \times 0.481 \times 35$$

$$= 18.75 + 200 + 250 + 1350 + 42.09$$

$$= 1.861 \times 10^3 \text{ cal}$$

So, heat required is 1861 calories.

(Heat)

10. $$V = 50 \times (10 \times 10^{-2}) = 5 \text{ m}^3$$

$$m = \rho V = 920 \times 5 = 4600 \text{ kg}$$

Heat required $= mL_f = 4600 \times 10^3 \times 80$

$$= 3.68 \times 10^8 \text{ cal}$$

$$= 1.541 \times 10^9 \text{ J}$$

Let t be the time to heat all of the ice into water at 0°C.

$$(200)t = 1.541 \times 10^9$$

$$t = 7.705 \times 10^6 \text{s} = 89.2 \text{ days}$$

Not a good idea.

(Heat)

11. Heat lost by steam = Heat gained by water and calorimeter cup

$$M_s L_v + M_s C_w (100 - 45) = M_w C_w (45 - 15) + M_c C_c (45 - 15)$$

$$M_s (540) + M_s \times 1(55) = 250 \times 1 \times 30 + 50 \times 0.215 \times 30$$

$$M_s (540 + 55) = 7500 + 322.5$$

$$M_s = \frac{7822.5}{595} = 13.15$$

Mass of steam absorbed is 13.1 g.

(Heat)

12. $$\frac{\Delta Q}{\Delta t} = \varepsilon \sigma A (T^4 - T'^4)$$

$$100 = 0.32 \times 5.67 \times 10^{-8} \times (45 \times 10^{-6})(T^4 - 295.15^4)$$

$$T^4 - 7.59 \times 10^9 = \frac{100}{8.165 \times 10^{-13}}$$

$$T^4 = 1.225 \times 10^{14} + 7.59 \times 10^9$$

T = 3326.7°K = 3053.6°C is the temperature of the filament.

(Radiation)

168 / Physics I

13. For heat flow by radiation,

$$\frac{\Delta Q}{\Delta t} = \varepsilon \sigma A(T^4 - T'^4)$$

$$= 1 \times 5.67 \times 10^{-8} \times (1.2 \times 10^{-4})(2373.15^4 - 297.15^4) = 215.7$$

Rate of heat loss is 215.7 W or 51.7 cal/s.

(Radiation)

14. For the double-pane window, we may consider 3 walls, glass-air-glass.

    The heat flow by conduction for N adjacent walls is:

$$\frac{\Delta Q}{\Delta t} = \frac{A(\Delta T)}{\left(\frac{\Delta x_1}{k_1}\right) + \left(\frac{\Delta x_2}{k_2}\right) + \ldots + \left(\frac{\Delta x_N}{k_N}\right)}$$

$$\frac{\Delta Q}{\Delta t} = \frac{0.75 \times 0.95 \times 38}{(3 \times 10^{-3}/0.84) + \left(\frac{3 \times 10^{-3}}{0.08}\right) + \left(\frac{3 \times 10^{-3}}{0.84}\right)}$$

$$\frac{\Delta Q}{\Delta t} = \frac{27.08 \times 10^{-2}}{3 \times 10^{-3}(14.88)}$$

$$= \frac{27.08}{4.46 \times 10^{-2}} = 607 \text{ W}$$

Heat loss is 544.8 W or 130 cal/s.

(Conduction)

15. Heat flow by conduction is:

$$\frac{\Delta Q}{\Delta t} = \frac{k_1 A(\Delta T)}{\Delta x_1} = \frac{k_2 A(\Delta T)}{\Delta x_2}$$

So, $\dfrac{k_1}{\Delta x_1} = \dfrac{k_2}{\Delta x_2}$

$$\Delta(x_2) = \frac{k_2}{k_1} \Delta x_1$$

$$= \frac{1.3}{4.14 \times 10^{-2}}(15 \times 10^{-2}) = 4.71 \text{ m}$$

Thickness of concrete has to be 4.71 m.

(Conduction)

16. Heat loss here is by convection.

    For convection processes:

    $$\frac{\Delta Q}{\Delta t} = hA(\Delta T)$$

    Here,

    $$h = 12 \text{ J/(m}^2\text{s}°\text{C)}$$

    $$A = 1.5 \text{ m}^2$$

    $$\Delta T = 10°\text{C}$$

    So,

    $$\frac{\Delta Q}{\Delta t} = 12 \times 1.5 \times 10 = 180 \text{ J/s}$$

    1 cal = 4.186 J

    $$\frac{\Delta Q}{\Delta t} = 43.0 \text{ cal/s} = 154.8 \text{ kcal/hr}$$

    Hence, (154.8 − 90) = 64.8 kcal/h enjoyable heat loss.

    (Convection)

17. (a) Total work done daily,

    $$\Delta W = 60 \times 8 + 400 \times 5 + 200 \times 3 + 100 \times 8 = 3880 \text{ kcal}$$

    Now, from 1st Law of Thermodynamics, $\Delta Q = \Delta U + \Delta W$

    ΔQ = Heat of food intake = 4500 kcal

    So, change in internal energy,

    $$\Delta U = \Delta Q - \Delta W = 4500 - 3880 = 620 \text{ kcal}$$

    (b) Let t be the time in hours for daily exercise.

    Then by condition of the problem,

    $$\Delta Q = \Delta U + \Delta W$$

    $$4500 = 60 \times 8 + 400 \times 5 + 200 \times 3 + 100(8 - t) + 1000t$$

    $$4500 = 3880 + 900t$$

    $$900t = 620$$

    $$t = 0.69 \text{ h}$$

    $$t = 41.3 \text{ minutes}$$

    (1st Law of Thermodynamics)

18. All of the heat goes to increase the internal energy of the water.

$$\Delta Q = \Delta U + \Delta W = \Delta U,$$

So, $\Delta U = \Delta Q = MC_w(\Delta T) = 75(4184)(25-10)$

$$\Delta U = 4.71 \times 10^6 \text{ Joules or}$$

$$\Delta U = 1125 \text{ kcal}$$

(1st Law of Thermodynamics)

19. Here the potential energy of the spring goes into heating the water and the lead.

$$\text{Potential Energy} = \frac{1}{2}kx^2 = \frac{1}{2} \times 450 \times 0.45^2 = 45.56 \text{ J}$$

Now, $\Delta Q = MC(\Delta T)$

$$45.56 = (1.2 \times 4184 + 0.75 \times 0.038)\Delta T$$

$$\Delta T = 9.07 \times 10^{-3} \text{ °K}$$

(1st Law of Thermodynamics)

20. (a) $\Delta Q = MC\Delta T = (10 \times 3.785)(4184)0.02 = 3.17 \times 10^3 \text{ J}$

$$\Delta U = \Delta Q = 3.17 \times 10^3 \text{ J or } 758 \text{ cal}$$

(b) Work done by motor in time t during heating,

$$\Delta W = (P)(t) = (1.5 \times 746 \times 0.2)t = 223.8t$$

So, $223.8t = 3.17 \times 10^3$

$$t = 14.16 \text{ s}$$

(1st Law of Thermodynamics)

21. From the 1st Law of Thermodynamics,

$$\Delta Q = \Delta U + \Delta W = \Delta U + p\Delta V$$

At constant volume,

$$\Delta V = 0$$

So, $(\Delta Q)_V = \Delta U$

$$= MC_V \Delta T$$

$$= 0.15 \times 0.75 \times (155 - 18)$$

$$\Delta U = 15.41 \text{ kcal}$$

When gas is heated at constant pressure,

$$(\Delta Q)_p = (\Delta U + \Delta W)$$

$$MC_p \Delta T = \Delta U + \Delta W$$

$$0.15 \times 1.15 \times 137 = 15.41 + \Delta W$$

$$\Delta W = 8.22 \text{ kcal} = 34.4 \text{ kJ}$$

(1st Law of Thermodynamics)

22. In this reversible process heat is slowly added to water to covert it into steam.

    Change in the entropy is:

    $$\Delta S = \frac{\Delta Q}{T} = \frac{mL_V}{T} \text{ (where } L_V \text{ is latent heat of vaporization)}$$

    $$\Delta S = \frac{(0.2)(540)}{373.15} = 0.289$$

    $$\Delta S = 0.289 \text{ kcal/}°K$$

    (2nd Law of Thermodynamics)

23. For Carnot's ideal engine, efficiency is:

    $$e = \left(1 - \frac{T_2}{T_1}\right), T_1 > T_2 \text{ (in degrees Kelvin)}$$

    $$e = \left(1 - \frac{423.15}{773.15}\right) = 1 - 0.55$$

    $$= 0.45$$

    (2nd Law of Thermodynamics)

24. The efficiency of Carnot's engine:

    $$e = \frac{T_1 - T_2}{T_1}$$

    Here, $T_1 = 1650 + 273 = 1923°K$

    $T_2 = 550 + 273 = 823°K$

    $$e = \frac{1923 - 823}{1923} = 0.57 = 57\%$$

    $$1 \text{ gal} = 3.785 \times 10^{-3} \text{ m}^3$$

    Mass of 1 gal $= 680 \times 3.785 \times 10^{-3} = 2.574$ kg

Heat produced = $2.574 \times 4.8 \times 10^7 = 1.24 \times 10^8$ J

Actual Efficiency, $e' = \dfrac{Q_{input}}{Q_{output}} = \dfrac{4.8 \times 10^7}{1.22 \times 10^8}$

$\qquad\qquad\qquad\quad = 0.39 = 39\%$

(2nd Law of Thermodynamics)

25. $\Delta Q = \Delta W = p_1 V_1 \ln \dfrac{V_2}{V_1}$

$\Delta S = \dfrac{\Delta Q}{T} = \dfrac{p_1 V_1}{T_1} \ln \dfrac{V_2}{V_1} = nR \ln \dfrac{V_2}{V_1}$

$\Delta S = \dfrac{m}{M} R \ln \dfrac{V_2}{V_1} = \dfrac{5}{28} \times (8314) \ln(0.25)$

$\Delta S = -2058$ J/°K

(2nd Law of Thermodynamics)

Grade Yourself

Circle the question numbers that you had incorrect. Then indicate the number of questions you missed. If you answered more than three questions incorrectly, you need to focus on that topic. (If a topic has less than three questions and you had at least one wrong, we suggest you study that topic also. Read your textbook, a review book, or ask your teacher for help.)

Subject: Temperature, Heat, and Thermodynamics

Topic	Question Numbers	Number Incorrect
Temperature	1, 2	
Thermal expansion	3, 4, 5, 6, 8	
Heat	7, 9, 10, 11	
Conduction	14, 15	
Convection	16	
Radiation	12, 13	
1st Law of Thermodynamics	17, 18, 19, 20, 21	
2nd Law of Thermodynamics	22, 23, 24, 25	

Vibrations and Wave Motion

Brief Yourself

Whenever there is a disturbance that repeats itself as time passes, it produces waves. Vibrations and waves are intimately connected.

Wave Motion:

The wave phenomenon is very common in our everyday life. Examples are water waves in the ocean, shock waves of an earthquake, radio waves from broadcasting stations, and microwave ovens in our kitchens. There are two kinds of waves; they are longitudinal waves and transverse waves.

If the wave moves in the same direction as the disturbance that produces the wave, it is called a *longitudinal wave*. If the disturbance moves in a direction perpendicular to the direction of the wave speed, it is called a *transverse wave*.

The period of vibration (T) is related to the frequency (f) of vibration as follows:

$$T = \frac{1}{f} \tag{1}$$

The unit of frequency is Hertz (Hz):

$1 \text{ Hz} = 1 \text{ cycle/second} = 1 \text{ s}^{-1}$.

The period and frequency of the wave are the same as the period and frequency of the vibration producing the wave. The distance between two adjacent peaks (crests) or dips (troughs) in a wave train is called the wavelength (λ) of the wave. The speed of the wave is:

$$v = \lambda f \tag{2}$$

The speed of a transverse wave produced on a stretched string or a wire is:

$v = [\text{(Tension in the string)/(Mass per unit length)}]^{1/2}$

i.e., $$v = \left[\frac{F}{\mu}\right]^{1/2} \tag{3}$$

Spherical Waves:

Waves from a point source propagate from the source in all directions as spherical surfaces (called wave fronts) at the speed of the wave. The ratio of the power of the spherical wave at one point compared to another is:

$$P_1/P_2 = (r_2/r_1)^2 \tag{4}$$

where P_1 and P_2 are the measured powers at distances r_1 and r_2 from the point source.

Standing Waves:

One or more waves may combine to produce a resultant wave. Two waves of the same frequency and amplitude, coming from opposite directions, may combine constructively to produce standing waves. The wavelength of such a standing wave is:

$$\lambda = \frac{2L}{n} \tag{5}$$

where n = 1, 2, 3, 4,... and L is the length over which the two waves combine.

Simple Harmonic Motion:

Simple harmonic motion is the most common and simple form of periodic motion. The familiar example is a mass attached to a spring undergoing vibrations. The restoring force (F) exerted by the spring undergoing simple harmonic motion is given by:

$$F = -kx \tag{6}$$

where k is the force constant of the spring and x is the amount of compression or expansion of the spring. The frequency of vibration is:

$$f = \frac{1}{2\pi}\sqrt{\frac{k}{m}} \tag{7}$$

where m is the mass of the weight attached to the spring. The total energy (E) of a vibrating mass-spring system is:

$$E = \frac{1}{2}mv^2 + \frac{1}{2}kx^2 \tag{8}$$

$$\text{Also, } E = \frac{1}{2}kA^2 = \frac{1}{2}mv_o^2 \tag{9}$$

Here, A = amplitude of vibration, v_o = maximum speed of the mass.

The instantaneous speed is:

$$v = v_o[1 - (x/A)^2] \tag{10}$$

Sound Waves:

Sound is the best example of a longitudinal wave. Sound waves propagate by compression and rarefaction of air. Sound waves cannot propagate in empty space. Our ear can hear sound waves in the frequency range of 20 Hz to 20 kHz. In an ideal gas of molecular mass M and absolute temperature T, the speed of sound is:

$$v = [\gamma RT/M]^{1/2} \tag{11}$$

Where γ is the ratio of specific heats c_p/c_v.

In a material medium, the speed of a sound wave is related to the modulus of elasticity and density of the medium.

$$v = [\text{Elastic Modulus/Density of the medium}]^{1/2} \tag{12}$$

The speed of sound in air at 0°C is 331 m/s. This speed increases with increasing temperature at a rate of 0.6 m/s for each °C above 0°C. Speed of sound in general has no dependence on frequency, wavelength, or pressure.

The intensity I, of a sound wave is measured as:

$$I = \frac{\text{Power}}{\text{Area}}$$

Loudness is a measure of human perception of sound. Loudness of sound increases with its intensity. The loudness level of a sound is measured in decibels (dB)

$$\text{Loudness level in dB} = 10 \log(I/I_o) \tag{13}$$

The zero of loudness level (I_o) is the weakest audible sound and is given by:

$$I_o = 1 \times 10^{-12} \text{ W/m}^2 \tag{14}$$

The normal ear can distinguish loudness levels that differ by as little as 1 dB.

Two sound waves of slightly different frequencies combine to produce a beat frequency, distinguishable by the high and low pitch fluctuations of the resultant sound. The frequency of beats is equal to the difference in the two frequencies of the sound waves.

Doppler Effect:

If there is a relative motion between the observer and the source of a sound, it results in the Doppler effect. When a sound source moving at a speed v_s approaches a listener moving at speed v_o toward the source, the listener will hear a higher frequency f given by:

$$f = f_o[(V + v_o)/(V - v_s)] \tag{15}$$

where the source emits sound at frequency f_o and the speed of sound in the medium is V. When a sound source moves at a speed v_s away from a listener moving at v_o away from the source, then the listener will hear a lower frequency f given by:

$$f = f_o[(V - v_o)/(V + v_s)] \tag{16}$$

Test Yourself

1. The frequency of certain red light is 4.7×10^{14} Hz, and the speed of light is 3×10^8 m/s.

   (a) What is the time period of this red light?
   (b) What is the wavelength of this red light?

2. The time period of the microwaves used in a physics experiment is 1.3×10^{-9} s. Find their frequency.

3. A radio station broadcasts at 88 MHz. What is the time period of these radio waves?

4. A watch spring vibrates at a frequency of 2.55 Hz. How long does it take to make 100 oscillations?

5. A guitar wire vibrates with a frequency of 6 Hz, producing transverse waves of wavelength 0.25 m. Find the speed of the wave.

6. A 5 m long string under tension produces transverse waves that move at a speed of 55 m/s. The mass of the string is 0.08 kg. What is the tension in the string?

7. The distance between the adjacent crests of transverse waves produced on a string is 0.25 m. Observation shows that 10 crests and 10 troughs pass through a given point every 15 s. Determine the wave speed.

8. The tension in a 20 m cord is 25 N. The speed of the transverse wave in the cord is 2.5 m/s. Find the total mass of the cord.

9. A piano string is under a tension of 1,500 N. Mass per unit length of the string is 0.007 kg/m. Find the velocity of the wave in the string.

10. A rope of mass 0.95 kg is stretched between two supports 25 m apart. The tension in the rope is 2,000 N. How long will a pulse take to travel from one support to the other?

11. An experiment shows that you require a sound intensity of 1.5 W/m² at a distance of 1 m from the speaker. What should be the power output of the speaker?

12. A 100 W electric lamp lights up a room. What is the intensity of light from this lamp at a distance of 2 m from it? Consider the light emitting filament to be a point source of light.

13. The speed of sound in air is 340 m/s. Find the wavelength and frequency of the fundamental and the first 2 overtones of sound waves in a 0.5 m long organ pipe, if the pipe has

    (a) two ends open
    (b) one end closed.

14. A string 2.5 m long is driven by a 260 Hz vibrator connected to its free end. The string resonates in 5 segments of loops. What are the wavelength and speed of the transverse wave?

15. Transverse waves travel in a string that resonates in three segments with a frequency of 450 Hz. What is the frequency that will cause it to vibrate in nine segments?

16. A string under tension and fastened at both ends resonates at 500 Hz and 550 Hz with no resonance in between. What is the fundamental resonance frequency?

17. A violin string of length 0.5 m resonates at its fundamental frequency of 200 Hz. Where along the wire should you place your finger to increase the fundamental frequency to 350 Hz?

18. A tuning fork with a frequency of 125 Hz is set to vibrating and held close to the mouth of a long tube closed at one end and filled with water. Transverse sound waves sent down the tube produce resonance at two successive water levels of 0.7 m and 2.1 m deep. Find the speed of the sound in air.

19. A pendulum clock made of a 1 m long string attached to a 0.25 kg mass is set oscillating. Find its time period and frequency.

20. A simple pendulum oscillates in a vertical plane with a maximum velocity of 2.5 m/s. How high will the attached mass rise from its lowest point?

21. In a mass-spring system, the displacement of the vibrating mass is:

    $x = 0.75\cos(5.6t)$ meter.

    The mass attached is 0.8 kg. Find the

    (a) amplitude of vibration
    (b) frequency of vibration
    (c) the force constant of the spring
    (d) the total energy of the system
    (e) potential energy and speed at T = 2 s.

22. A scale in a fish market vibrates at 2.5 Hz when a fish of mass 1.5 kg is placed on it. What is the spring constant?

23. A scale in the supermarket stretches 5 cm from its relaxed position when vegetables of mass 0.75 kg are placed on it. What will be the frequency of vibration if 1.0 kg of potatoes are placed on it and removed?

24. You hear a thunder clap 15 s after you see lightning on a stormy night. The average speed of the sound wave in the air is 343 m/s. How far are you from the lightning stroke? The speed of light is 3×10^8 m/s.

25. Calculate the power level of a sound in decibels (dB) if the intensity of the sound is 5 microwatt/m^2.

26. The density of aluminum is 2.7×10^3 kg/m^3 and its Young's modulus is 7×10^{10} N/m^2. Find the speed of sound in the aluminum.

27. The sound level of a vacuum cleaner is listed as 50 dB. What will be its intensity in W/m^2?

28. In a firework display, an observer hears the sound of explosion from an exploding rocket 500 m away. What is the time after the explosion that the observer will hear it? The temperature of the air is 15°C.

29. A physicist at a rock concert 25 m from the audio speaker finds the sound level to be 100 dB. How should he advise others if they wanted to hear no less than 80 dB of music from the same speaker? Ignore absorption of sound in the air.

30. Sound waves at a frequency of 975 Hz are emitted uniformly in all directions. An observer sitting 3 m from the source measures a loudness level of 36 dB. Calculate the power of sound at the emitting source.

31. The engine of a commuter train moving at 20 m/s, sounds its horn at a frequency of 375 Hz. What will be the frequency observed by a person standing on the station platform if the train is,

    (a) approaching the observer?
    (b) receding from the observer?

    The speed of sound is 341 m/s.

32. A police car moving at 90 mph starts chasing a speeding car with its siren set at 1,500 Hz. The driver of the speeding car measures the frequency of the siren to be 1,850 Hz. If the speed limit is 65 mph, was the driver speeding? Speed of sound is 341 m/s.

Check Yourself

1. (a) Time period,

$$T = \frac{1}{f}, \quad f = 4.7 \times 10^{14} \text{ Hz}$$

$$T = \frac{1}{4.7 \times 10^{14}} = 2.13 \times 10^{-15} \text{ s}$$

(b) Speed, $\quad v = \lambda f$

Wavelength, $\lambda = \dfrac{v}{f} = \dfrac{3\times 10^8}{4.7\times 10^{14}}$

$\lambda = 6.38\times 10^{-7}$ m

(Waves in general)

2. $\quad T = \dfrac{1}{f},$

So, frequency $f = \dfrac{1}{T} = \dfrac{1}{1.3\times 10^{-9}}$

$f = 7.69\times 10^8$ Hz = 769 MHz

(Waves in general)

3. $\quad T = \dfrac{1}{f} = \dfrac{1}{88\times 10^6} = 1.14\times 10^{-8}$ s

(Waves in general)

4. $\qquad f = 2.55$ Hz

$T = \dfrac{1}{f} = \dfrac{1}{2.55} = 0.392$

Time of one oscillation = 0.392 s

Time for 100 oscillations = 0.392 × 100

= 39.2 s

(Waves in general)

5. Speed,

$v = \lambda f = 0.25 \times 6 = 1.5$ m/s

(Waves in general)

6. $\quad v = \sqrt{\dfrac{\text{Tension}}{\text{Mass/unit length}}} = \sqrt{\dfrac{F}{\mu}}$

$v^2 = \dfrac{F}{\mu}$

$F = \mu v^2$

Here, $\mu = \dfrac{0.08}{5} = 0.016$ kg/m and $v = 55$ m/s

So, $F = 0.016 \times 55^2$

$F = 48.4\,\text{N}$

(Transverse waves)

7. Here, wavelength

   $\lambda = 0.25\,\text{m}$

   Frequency, $f = \dfrac{\text{\# of waves}}{\text{Time}} = \dfrac{10}{15} = 0.67\,\text{Hz}$

   Speed, $v = \lambda f = 0.25 \times 0.67 = 1.67 \times 10^{-1} = 16.7\,\text{cm/s}$

(Waves in general)

8. $v = \sqrt{\dfrac{F}{\mu}},\quad v^2 = \dfrac{F}{\mu}$

   $\mu = \dfrac{F}{v^2}$

   $\dfrac{m}{l} = \dfrac{F}{v^2}$

   $m = l\left(\dfrac{F}{v^2}\right) = 20\left(\dfrac{25}{2.5^2}\right)$

   Total Mass = 80 kg

(Transverse waves)

9. $v = \sqrt{\dfrac{F}{\mu}} = [1500/0.007]^{1/2} = 4.63 \times 10^2\,\text{m/s}$

(Transverse waves)

10. $v = \sqrt{\dfrac{F}{\mu}},\ F = 2000\,\text{N},\ \mu = \dfrac{0.95}{25}$

    $\mu = 3.8 \times 10^{-2}\,\text{kg/m}$

    $v = \left[\dfrac{2000}{3.8 \times 10^{-2}}\right]^{1/2} = 2.29 \times 10^2\,\text{m/s}$

    $v = \dfrac{\Delta x}{\Delta t}$

    $\Delta t = \Delta x / v = 25/2.29 \times 10^2$

    $= 0.11\,\text{s}$

(Transverse waves)

11. Spherical surface at 1 m from the speaker = $4\pi r^2 = 4\pi(1)^2 = 12.57$ m^2

Intensity, $I = \dfrac{\text{Power}}{\text{Area}} = \dfrac{P}{A}$

$P = IA = (1.5)12.57 = 18.8$ Watts

Total power at a distance of one meter is the same as power emitted by the speaker.

So, power output of the speaker = 18.8 W

(Spherical waves)

12. Spherical surface area of radius 2 m is,

$A = 4\pi r^2 = 4\pi(2)^2 = 16\pi = 50.3$ m^2

Intensity,

$I = \dfrac{P}{A} = \dfrac{100}{50.3}$

$I = 1.99$ W/m^2

(Spherical waves)

13. (a) For both ends open,

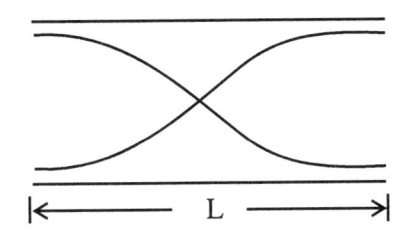

$\lambda_n = \dfrac{2L}{n}, \quad n = 1, 2, 3, \ldots$

= number of nodes

Fundamental wavelength and frequency,

$\lambda_1 = \dfrac{2 \times 0.5}{1} = 1$ m

$f_1 = \dfrac{v}{\lambda_1} = \dfrac{340}{1} = 340$ Hz

For first overtone, $n = 2$

$\lambda_2 = \dfrac{2L}{n} = \dfrac{2L}{2} = L = 0.5$ m

$$f_2 = \frac{v}{\lambda_2} = \frac{340}{0.5} = 680\,\text{Hz}$$

For second overtone,

$$\lambda_3 = \frac{2L}{n} = \frac{2L}{3} = \frac{2}{3} \times 0.5 = 0.33\,\text{m}$$

$$f_3 = \frac{v}{\lambda_3} = \frac{340}{0.33} = 1020\,\text{Hz}$$

(b) For one end closed,

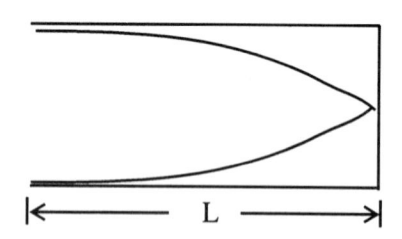

$$\lambda_n = \frac{4L}{2n+1},$$

n = number of nodes = 0, 1, 2, 3, 4, ...

For fundamental wavelength and frequency $n = 0$,

$$\lambda_1 = \frac{4L}{1} = 4 \times 0.5 = 2\,\text{m}$$

$$f_1 = \frac{v}{\lambda} = \frac{340}{2} = 170\,\text{Hz}$$

For first overtone, $n = 1$,

$$\lambda_2 = \frac{4L}{2 \times 1 + 1} = \frac{4L}{3} = \frac{4 \times 0.5}{3} = 0.667$$

$$\lambda_2 = 0.67\,\text{m}$$

and $$f_2 = \frac{v}{\lambda_2} = \frac{340}{0.667} = 510\,\text{Hz}$$

For second overtone, $n = 2$,

$$\lambda_3 = \frac{4L}{2 \times 2 + 1} = \frac{4L}{5} = \frac{4 \times 0.5}{5}$$

$$\lambda_3 = 0.4\,\text{m}$$

$$f_3 = \frac{v}{\lambda_3} = \frac{340}{0.4} = 850\,\text{Hz}$$

(Standing waves)

14. $\qquad L = 2.5\,\text{m},\ f = 260\,\text{Hz}$

    $5 \text{ segments} = 5\left(\frac{\lambda}{2}\right) = L$

    Therefore, $\lambda = \dfrac{2L}{5} = \dfrac{2 \times 2.5}{5} = 1$

    $v = \lambda f = 1 \times 260 = 260\,\text{m/s}$

(Transverse waves)

15. Here, for three segments,

    $3\left(\dfrac{\lambda}{2}\right) = L$

    So, $\lambda_3 = \dfrac{2L}{3}$ \hfill (1)

    For nine segments,

    $9\left(\dfrac{\lambda}{2}\right) = L$

    $\lambda_9 = \dfrac{2L}{9}$ \hfill (2)

    Now, $v = \lambda f$

    So, $f_1 \lambda_1 = f_2 \lambda_2 = f_3 \lambda_3 = v = \text{constant}$

    So, $f_3 \lambda_3 = f_9 \lambda_9$ using equations (1) and (2)

    $(450)\dfrac{2L}{3} = f_9\left(\dfrac{2L}{9}\right)$

    $f_9 = \dfrac{450 \times 9}{3} = 1350\,\text{Hz}$

(Standing waves)

16. Frequency,

    $f = \dfrac{v}{\lambda}$

    $f_n = \dfrac{v}{\lambda_n}$ \hfill (1)

For both ends fixed,

$$\lambda_n = \frac{2L}{n}, n = 1, 2, 3 \qquad (2)$$

i.e., $x_1 = 2L$

using equation (2) in equation (1) we get,

$$f_n = \frac{v}{2L/n} = n\left(\frac{v}{2L}\right) = n\left(\frac{v}{\lambda_1}\right)$$

$$f_n = nf_1$$

Also, $f_{n+1} = (n+1)f_1$

Subtracting, $f_{n+1} - f_n = f_1$

That is, $550 - 500 = f_1$

Fundamental frequency, $f_1 = 50\,\text{Hz}$

(Transverse waves)

17. For standing waves,

    $$\lambda_n = \frac{2L}{n}, n = 1, 2, 3$$

    For fundamental wavelength

    $$\lambda_1 = \frac{2L}{1}$$

    And fundamental frequency,

    $$f_1 = \frac{v}{\lambda_1} = \frac{v}{2L}$$

    So, $\dfrac{f_1}{f'_1} = \dfrac{v/2L}{v/2L'} = \dfrac{L'}{L}$

    $$L' = \frac{f_1}{f'_1}L = \frac{200}{350}(0.5) = 0.286\,\text{m}$$

    $L' = 28.6\,\text{cm}$

    The finger must shorten the length to 28.6 cm.

    (Standing waves)

18.

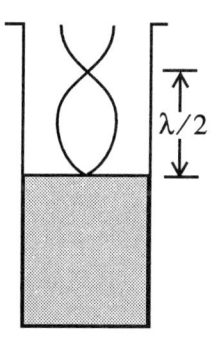

Here, wavelength of sound waves is,

$$\frac{\lambda}{2} = (2.1 - 0.7) = 1.4 \text{ m}$$

$$\lambda = 2.8 \text{ m}$$

(Transverse waves)

19. The time period of a simple pendulum is,

$$T = 2\pi\sqrt{\frac{l}{g}} = 6.28\left[\frac{1}{9.81}\right]^{1/2} = 2.01 \text{ s}$$

$$f = \frac{1}{T} = 0.498 \text{ Hz}$$

(Simple harmonic motion)

20. Total energy must be conserved.

Total energy,

$$E = \frac{1}{2}mv_{max}^2 = mgh_{max}$$

So, $\frac{1}{2}v_{max}^2 = gh_{max}$

$$h_{max} = \frac{v_{max}^2}{2g} = \frac{2.5^2}{2 \times 9.81} = 0.32 \text{ m}$$

So, the attached mass will rise 32 cm from its lowest point.

(Simple harmonic motion)

21. (a) $x = 0.75 \cos(5.6t)$ must be compared with the known expression for displacement of a wave,

$$x = x_o \cos(\omega t)$$

So, amplitude is 0.75 m.

(b) Here, $\omega = 5.6$

$$f = \frac{\omega}{2\pi} = \frac{5.6}{2\pi} = 0.89 \text{ Hz}$$

(c) The force constant of the spring is related to the frequency by the following expression,

$$\omega = \sqrt{\frac{k}{m}}, \quad \omega^2 = \frac{k}{m}$$

$$k = m\omega^2 = 0.8(5.6)^2 = 25.1$$

Force constant is 25.1 N/m.

(d) Total energy $E = KE + PE$

$$E = \frac{1}{2}mv^2 + \frac{1}{2}kx^2$$

For maximum potential energy,

$$E = \frac{1}{2}kA^2 \text{ where } A \text{ is the amplitude of vibration.}$$

$$E = \frac{1}{2}(25.1)(0.75)^2 = 7.1 \text{ J is the total energy.}$$

(e) At $t = 2\text{ s}$

$$x = 0.75\cos[(5.6)(2)] = 0.75\cos(11.2) = 0.152 \text{ m}$$

Potential Energy, $PE = \frac{1}{2}kx^2 = \frac{1}{2}(25.1)(0.152)^2 = 0.29 \text{ J}$

Kinetic Energy, $KE = E - PE = 7.1 - 0.29 = 6.81 \text{ J}$

$$\frac{1}{2}mv^2 = 6.81$$

$$v^2 = \frac{2}{m}(6.81)$$

$$v = \sqrt{\frac{2 \times 6.81}{0.8}} = 4.13 \text{ m/s}$$

(Simple harmonic motion)

22. $\omega = \sqrt{\frac{k}{m}}, \quad k = m\omega^2 = m(2\pi f)^2$

$$k = 4\pi^2 m f^2 = 4\pi^2 \times 1.5 \times (2.5)^2 = 370.1 \text{ N/m}$$

Spring constant is 370.1 N/m

(Simple harmonic motion)

23. From Hooke's law of force,

$$F = -kx$$

Ignoring the negative sign for the magnitude of the force,

$$mg = kx$$

$$k = \frac{mg}{x} = \frac{0.75 \times 9.81}{0.05} = 147.1 \text{ N/m}$$

Again, $\omega = \sqrt{\frac{k}{m}}$

$$k = m\omega^2 = m(2\pi f)^2 = 4\pi^2 m f^2$$

$$147.1 = 4\pi^2 \times 1.0 \times f^2$$

$$f = \sqrt{\frac{147.1}{4\pi^2}} = \frac{1}{2\pi}\sqrt{147.1} = 1.93 \text{ Hz}$$

(Simple harmonic motion)

24. Let the distance be x. Let t be the time taken by light to travel to the observer.

$$x = ct = v(t + 15)$$

$$3 \times 10^8 t = 343(t + 15) = 343t + 5145$$

$$t = 1.715 \times 10^{-5} \text{ s}$$

So, $x = ct = 3 \times 10^8 \times 1.715 \times 10^{-5}$

$$x = 5145 \text{ m}$$

(Waves in general)

25. Level of sound in decibel is

$$dB = 10 \times \log\left(\frac{I}{I_0}\right)$$

where $I_0 = 1 \times 10^{-12}$ w/m²

Here, $I = 5 \times 10^{-6}$ w/m²

$$dB = 10\log(5 \times 10^{-6}/1 \times 10^{-12})$$

$$= 10\log(5 \times 10^6)$$

= 67, So, the power level is 67 dB.

(Sound waves)

26. Speed of sound is

    $$v = \sqrt{(\text{Modulus of elasticity}/\text{Density of medium})}$$

    $$v = [Y/P]^{1/2} = [7\times10^{10}/2.7\times10^3]^{1/2}$$

    $$v = 5.1\times10^3$$

    $$v = 5100 \text{ m/s}$$

(Sound waves)

27. Sound level of vacuum cleaner = 50 dB

    $$50 = 10\log\left(\frac{I}{I_0}\right)$$

    $$5 = \log\left(\frac{I}{I_0}\right)$$

    $$\frac{I}{I_0} = 10^5$$

    So, $I = I_0 \times 10^5 = 1\times10^{-12} \times 10^5 = 1\times10^{-7}$ w/m^2

    $$I = 0.1 \mu W/m^2$$

(Sound waves)

28. For temperature dependence of the speed of sound we have

    $$v \propto \sqrt{T}$$

    So, $\dfrac{v}{v_0} = \sqrt{\dfrac{T}{T_0}}$

    $$v = v_0(T/T_0)^{\frac{1}{2}} = 331\left(\frac{288}{273}\right)^{\frac{1}{2}}$$

    $$v = 340 \text{ m/s}$$

    $$x = vt$$

    $$t = \frac{x}{v} = \frac{500}{340} = 1.47 \text{ s}$$

Vibrations and Wave Motion / 189

The explosion takes place at about the same time the firework is seen. The sound is heard 1.47 s after seeing the firework.

(Sound waves)

29. $$100 = 10 \times \log\left(\frac{I}{I_0}\right)$$

So, $I_1 = I_0(10^{10}) = 1 \times 10^{-12} \times 10^{10} = 1 \times 10^{-2}\,W/m^2$

$$80 = 10 \times \log\left(\frac{I}{I_0}\right)$$

$I_2 = I_0(10^8) = 1 \times 10^{-12} \times 10^8 = 1 \times 10^{-4}\,W/m^2$

Intensity decreases as $\frac{1}{r^2}$. That is, $I \propto \frac{1}{r^2}$

So, $\frac{I_1}{I_2} = \left(\frac{r_2}{r_1}\right)^2$

$r_2^2 = r_1^2\left(\frac{I_1}{I_2}\right) = \frac{25^2 \times 10^{-2}}{1 \times 10^{-4}} = 6.25 \times 10^4$

$r_2 = 250\,m$

So, he should advise others to remain within 250 m of the speaker.

(Spherical waves)

30. Intensity does not depend on frequency.

$$36 = 10 \times \log\left(\frac{I}{I_0}\right),\ I = I_0(10^{3.6}) = 1 \times 10^{-12} \times 4 \times 10^3$$

Total Power, $P = I(4\pi r^2) = (4 \times 10^{-9})4\pi(3)^2$

$P = 4.5 \times 10^{-7}\,W$ or $0.45\,\mu W$

(Spherical waves)

31. (a) This is a Doppler effect case.

$$f = f_0\left(\frac{v + v_0}{v - v_S}\right)$$

$$f = 375\left(\frac{341 + 0}{341 - 20}\right) = 398.4\,Hz$$

(b) $f = f_0\left(\frac{v - v_0}{v + v_S}\right) = 375\left(\frac{341}{341 + 20}\right) = 354.2$

$f = 354.2\,\text{Hz}$

(Doppler effect)

32. Here the observer hears sound at an increased frequency. So, the source must be approaching the observer. The driver is the observer and police car the source of sound.

$$\frac{f}{f_0} = \frac{v + v_0}{v - v_S}$$

$$\frac{1850}{1500} = \frac{341 + v_0}{341 - (90 \times 0.447)}$$

$$1.23 = 341 + v_0$$

$$v_0 = 29\,\text{m/s} = 64.9\,\text{mph}$$

So, he was not speeding.

(Doppler effect)

Grade Yourself

Circle the question numbers that you had incorrect. Then indicate the number of questions you missed. If you answered more than three questions incorrectly, you need to focus on that topic. (If a topic has less than three questions and you had at least one wrong, we suggest you study that topic also. Read your textbook, a review book, or ask your teacher for help.)

Subject: Vibrations and Wave Motion

Topic	Question Numbers	Number Incorrect
Waves in general	1, 2, 3, 4, 5, 7, 24	
Transverse waves	6, 8, 9, 10, 14, 16, 18	
Spherical waves	11, 12, 29, 30	
Standing waves	13, 15, 17	
Simple harmonic motion	19, 20, 21, 22, 23	
Sound waves	25, 26, 27, 28	
Doppler effect	31, 32	